THE ULTIMATE GUIDE TO BUYING AND SELLING COOPS AND CONDOS IN NEW YORK CITY

THE ULTIMATE GUIDE TO
Buying and Selling
Coops and Condos
IN NEW YORK CITY

BY **NEIL J. BINDER**

ISBN 0-9679249-2-8
1. Real Estate 2. New York City 3. Business

Published by Nice Idea Publishing, Inc.
c/o Bellmarc Companies
352 Park Avenue South, 9th Floor, New York, N.Y. 10010

*I wish to dedicate this book to all the Bellmarc salespeople.
It has been the greatest honor of my life to have been associated with
each and every one of you.*

ACKNOWLEDGEMENTS

While preparing this book, I relied on many people to review my drafts and make suggestions that have resulted in a much finer end product than I ever could have produced on my own. First, I would like to thank my business partner, Marc Broxmeyer, for his lucid comments and encouragement. Second, I would like to thank all of the managers of the Bellmarc offices for their excellent advice: Lisa Strobing, Sales Manager of the Gramercy/Chelsea Office; Ron Tardanico, Sales Manager of the East Side Office; Janice Silver, Sales Manager of the Midtown Office; Veronica Raehse, Sales Manager of the Greenwich Village Office; John Lawrence, Sales Manager of the Lincoln Center Area Office; Ken Scheff, Sales Manager of the West Side Office; and John Janangelo, President of Property Management.

I also sought assistance from professionals whose expertise in their specialties I especially respect. I would like to thank Dan Levitan, of Home Mortgage Acceptance Corp. (HMAC), for his advice in the area of mortgages; Rick Glass, CPA, of Glass and Bloom CPAs, for his assistance in tax and accounting matters; and Dennis Greenstein, Esq., of Greenstein, Starr, Gerstein & Rinaldi, LLP for reviewing the legal aspects of the book. The number of people who gave me editorial assistance includes Betsy Malcolm, Margaret Daisley, and Joe Polivy.

While she is at the bottom of this page, her efforts really warrant that she be at the top. My deepest gratitude to Nina Scerbo of Nina Scerbo Design Inc., whose care and diligence in every aspect of this work, including the creation of an excellent design, make it more than mere words.

Table of Contents

Introduction

Marc Broxmeyer and I never expected to enter the real estate brokerage business together. It was by chance that we met at a luncheon in 1979, held by the Real Estate Board of New York for young real estate professionals, where we sat at the same table and shared our experiences.

Marc grew up in Hicksville, Long Island, with his mother and stepfather in modest surroundings. His parents had divorced when he was young, and his father became successful in real estate ventures in Florida. After Marc came of age, he joined his father in this burgeoning business which failed in 1973 when a severe recession caused the house of cards to collapse. At that point, Marc left Florida and returned to New York. Never having graduated college, he decided to get an accounting degree at New York University. He also decided to use his remaining limited funds, and what he could borrow from family members, to buy a small apartment building in Bell Harbor, Queens. In doing so, he formed a corporation, combining his first name and that of Bell Harbor into "Bellmarc."

My own experience contrasted with Marc's in many ways. I grew up in a middle-income environment in Beechhurst, Queens. I graduated from Syracuse University, where I was an Honors student majoring in Domestic Government and Law, and received my MBA in Finance from New York University's Graduate School of Business. After a brief stint at Arthur Andersen & Co. as an accountant, I obtained my CPA and became associated with a small group of entrepreneurs working on real estate partnerships.

At the time we met, Marc and I were both looking for an opportunity. I saw in Marc a practical businessman with "street smarts" who knew how to manage residential properties. Marc saw in me a proficient finance technician with considerable knowledge of real estate. I suggested the first investment opportunity, and though Marc decided against it, he came up with an alternate proposal a few weeks later. He described a small apartment building in Bell Harbor, Queens, not far from the property he already owned. Initially, I was hesitant because of the distance from Manhattan, which I considered to be my core market area. However, I discussed the property with my father who, after seeing it and speaking with Marc, was willing to invest. His interest stimulated my enthusiasm.

Marc needed $150,000 in cash to buy the property. He had $75,000 from his family and was looking for $75,000 from me. After satisfying myself that it was, indeed, a property worth buying, we signed the contract the next day.

I became partners with someone I had met only once over lunch! We had no formal agreement, nor any understanding about how we were going to conduct our business affairs. We just shook hands and that was it.

Soon afterward, we began looking for our next investment opportunity, but the New York City real estate market had changed. This was the end of 1979 and "the Big Apple" was on the verge of bankruptcy. Interest rates were skyrocketing, oil prices were going through the roof, and no one wanted to invest in an uncertain economic environment.

Marc and I had rented a small office in Greenwich Village, which we filled with recycled furniture. We each smoked two packs of cigarettes a day, ate dark-meat turkey sandwiches at our desks, and pondered what to do given our predicament. In a nutshell, our future looked bleak. It was Marc who came up with the idea of real estate brokerage. He felt that cooperative apartments were the future, and that the prospects in this market niche were excellent.

Initially, I didn't agree. Then, a friend of Marc's asked if he could work in our office under Marc's real estate brokerage license. I said okay, and we became partners in this endeavor as well. Marc took the friend under his wing and watched as he labored at the business with no success.

One night, Marc told his protégé, "You've been working at this for months, and you haven't done one deal. Give me the name of one of your prospects. Maybe I can work something out." Marc made the call, and quickly made a deal. When he hung up, he looked at me and smiled. "Your turn," he said. I made a call to another prospect, and I too made a deal. We took turns until we completed seven offers and acceptances that night. When we finally called it quits for the evening, we went out to celebrate — lobsters, beer, the works!

The next day, six of the seven deals fell through. But one remained solid, proving that this was a business worth investing our efforts in. Because of our limited resources, we decided to use the company Marc had previously formed rather than take on the cost of another incorporation. The name "Bellmarc" sounded pretty good to us — a lot better than "Binder and Broxmeyer" or "Broxmeyer and Binder" or, heaven help us, "BroxBind."

From the start, we specialized. At the time, most residential brokerage firms were handling rentals as well as sales, and were centralized in mid-Manhattan. We opted to specialize in cooperative apartment sales in Greenwich Village. This gave us a decisive advantage, since we were closer to the properties we were selling than our competitors were, and knew the market better.

We also recognized that many real estate agents attempting to serve the emerging cooperative apartment sales market were poorly equipped to handle its technical and legal demands. Accordingly, a second feature of our business model became training. Our training program became a way to both recruit and develop a base of good salespeople. Initially, Bellmarc had nothing attractive to offer an ambitious salesperson over the competition. But once we implemented a training program, we gained an edge.

A substantial part of my professional career for over twenty years has been dedicated to training. The original program I developed arose from my discussions with new salespeople, and consisted of a series of audio tapes. But the real estate market is never static, and I found myself having to make more tapes as new issues appeared.

After completing eighteen tapes, I saw the need for another training device, so I wrote a sales manual, which eventually grew to over 500 pages. Then, to insure that trainees took the material seriously, I instituted two four-hour written exams, plus two rigorous take-home tests, each requiring approximately 25 pages of work. Still, the sales managers complained about the trainees' lack of preparation. So I developed a series of 18 two-hour seminars on selling and negotiating techniques.

The current Bellmarc Training Program takes two months of intensive work to complete. Nearly one-third of the entering trainees never make it through. The remaining two-thirds become very effective salespeople, with 75% staying in the industry for the long term, earning successful incomes. Many have purchased beautiful homes, taken exotic vacations, and bought luxury cars. They have been rewarded for their efforts in countless ways. My greatest reward has been their success.

Bellmarc's training program is frequently acknowledged to be the best in the real estate industry. This book represents the next logical step. Just as I teach salespeople, there are many things I can do to help a buyer, seller, or interested third party better understand the world of cooperatives and condominiums in New York City.

This book is designed to be the ultimate guide: a good overview of what you need to know about buying and selling coops and condos in New York City; a reference guide to walk you through the specifics of each stage of the process; a guide to pertinent terminology; and an introduction to the basics of real estate investing. Whatever your purpose is in reading it, I hope it provides you with the help you need.

The Purchasing Journey

An overview of the process of buying a home

STEP 1
SUBMITTING THE BID

As far as the seller is concerned, the sales price, in the vast majority of cases, is "all cash." That means the seller will receive a check for the full amount on the day of the closing. About 75% of the time, the buyer will need a loan (mortgage) from a bank in order to have enough money to complete the transaction. If you need a mortgage, your offer is conditional upon your loan being approved by a lending institution. Your purchase offer is considered an **Offer Subject To Financing**.

It is often possible to get a mortgage pre-approved by a bank before actually finding a specific property. Always make sure the pre-approval is in writing and that it is not subject to any conditions you can't realistically meet. The advantage of a pre-approved loan is that it may no longer be necessary to submit an offer subject to any conditions. An **Unconditional Offer** is one in which financing is guaranteed by the buyer, or where only equity capital will be used to complete the purchase.

Being able to make an unconditional offer puts the buyer in an advantageous negotiating position since the buyer can offer greater certainty for the successful conclusion of the transaction. Sellers are often willing to take a lower price in exchange for this certainty. However, even if an offer is unconditional, the coop contract still makes the transaction contingent on the cooperative board approving the apartment purchase. In a condominium, a "right of first refusal" procedure may be required.

When something is physically wrong with the apartment — such as a broken fixture or damaged ceiling — a buyer might submit an offer **Subject to Correction**. That is, the offer is only good in the event that the seller cures the offensive condition.

Buyers should consider what items they would like to have included in the transaction. Normally, it is understood by everyone that kitchen cabinets and appliances are included in the sale. But misunderstandings frequently occur regarding almost every other item in the apartment. Air conditioners, light fixtures, blinds and drapes, furnishings, and built-ins should be expressly stated as included or not included with any offer.

A **Verbal Offer** creates no legal obligation for either the buyer or the seller. Therefore, if you submit an offer, you are free to change your mind until you sign a contract. Some buyers are hesitant to make an offer significantly lower than the seller's asking price. Nothing is lost by submitting a low offer and there may be much to be gained. A good real estate broker will tell you that, in most instances, as long as there is reasonable justification for the offer, it will be seriously considered.

STEP 2
THE CONTRACT PROCEDURE

Once the basic terms of the deal have been agreed to, you should immediately notify your attorney. It is advisable to choose an attorney who has significant experience with real estate transactions in New York City. Getting a few recommendations from a real estate broker or a mortgage broker may be helpful.

The contract is usually prepared by the seller's attorney and sent to the buyer's attorney, who reviews it along with the building's prospectus, the cooperative corporation's or condominium association's last financial report, and other pertinent documents. The attorney's purpose is to insure that all material issues are identified and properly addressed with the client, the buyer. If the contract is acceptable, the buyer signs it and submits a check for 10% of the contract price as a **Deposit**. Normally, multiple copies of the contract are signed, so that both the buyer and the seller have original documents. Once the contracts are signed by the buyer, they are sent to the seller's attorney along with the deposit check.

The seller's attorney places the deposit funds into an **Escrow Account** (a special bank account held in trust for the parties to the transaction), and arranges for the seller's signature. The seller's attorney will then send an original set of fully-executed contracts to the buyer's attorney. A **Legally Binding Contract** is now in full force, since it has been signed by both parties and delivered to each.

STEP 3
GETTING A MORTGAGE

A mortgage is a loan that uses real estate as security. If you don't pay the loan according to the terms of your agreement, the bank can take your real estate as an alternate form of repaying the debt (foreclosure). Obviously, it is essential that you not borrow more than you can afford.

In the case of a cooperative apartment, you are not buying real estate. You are buying stock in a corporation that owns the building and receiving a proprietary lease entitling you to reside in a specific apartment. Since you own shares in a coop, not real estate, your loan is not technically considered a mortgage. Rather, it is a **Financing Loan**. Notwithstanding this technicality, the general public, and even brokers, use the term "mortgage" to include a loan for a coop apartment. There are various types of mortgages, or financing loans, that are available. They fall into two predominant categories: variable rate loans and fixed rate loans.

With a **Variable Rate Loan**, the rate of interest changes within a short period of time, usually one, two, or three years. Recently, there have even been loans offered which vary monthly. The loan also calls for the related monthly payment to vary periodically either up or down, based on an index, such as the United States Treasury Bill Rate. Usually, there is a "cap" on this interest rate variation — generally two percentage points in any given adjustment period.

The advantage of a variable rate loan is that your interest rate at inception is normally one or two percent less than the rate on a fixed rate loan. Since your payment also is initially less, the bank will permit you to borrow more money than with a fixed rate mortgage. The disadvantage is that you are subject to greater economic risk in the future. Frequently, when interest rates rise the economy slows. Therefore, you may wind up getting an increase in your monthly mortgage payment at the same time your finances are tightening.

A **Fixed Rate Loan** provides for an unvarying monthly payment for the term of the loan, usually 15 or 30 years. This is valuable to people who are looking to maintain a predictable monthly budget since this type of loan eliminates the risk of being subject to a change in the payment. However, the reverse is also true, there is no opportunity to have a lower payment if interest rates decline.

As a general rule, a variable rate loan appears preferable to buyers who anticipate five years or less of ownership and a fixed rate loan appears preferable to those who have a longer time horizon.

It is useful to seek the advice of a reputable **Mortgage Broker** for assistance in getting a loan. A mortgage broker can present you with an array of programs offered by many different banks on a competitive basis. This improves the likelihood that you will find the best rate and terms in the marketplace. Many buyers have found that going directly to their bank, even if they have an excellent banking relationship, affords them no better terms and conditions than those offered through a mortgage broker. In addition, a mortgage broker will assist you in preparing all the necessary documents and explain any aspects of the process that are unclear. The best part about this service is that it is free to the buyer. The mortgage broker's commission is paid by the bank lending the funds.

In obtaining a mortgage, the buyer will incur certain **Up Front Costs** including an application fee, an appraisal fee (to verify the value of the property), the bank's legal fees (for preparing and processing loan documents), and "points" (additional profit to the bank).

STEP 4
THE BOARD APPROVAL PROCESS

A lot has been made in the press about a ritual many New York City home buyers endure when purchasing an apartment in a cooperative building — the coop board review process. In reality, the board review is rarely as offensive as the news reports have made it out to be. In most instances, it is more about getting to know you, and welcoming you into the coop community, than about making your life miserable. In our overall experience, board rejections are somewhat rare. However, there are some material issues you should be aware of when applying for approval.

Boards will **reject** applicants primarily for the following reasons:

1. *You do not meet the minimum cash equity requirement set forth for the building, or your financial information does not show evidence of income adequate to support your purchase.*
2. *You have a pet and there is a no-pet rule.*
3. *You have been dishonest or deceptive in your application material.*
4. *You present yourself at the interview in an abusive, suspicious, or offensive manner rather than acting open and friendly.*

The following are normally **required documents** for a **Board Package**:

1. *An application with basic information about yourself, including your financial condition.*
2. *One or two years' tax returns.*
3. *Two to four letters of personal reference.*
4. *Two to four reference letters from people you work with.*
5. *One letter from a former landlord (if applicable), affirming you were a good tenant.*
6. *One letter from a bank, affirming your balances and how long you have had an account with the bank.*
7. *One letter from your employer, affirming your position and length of employment and your salary, including bonuses (if applicable).*
8. *Your contract of sale.*
9. *Your mortgage commitment letter.*
10. *Various documentation supporting your represented financial condition.*

Customarily, the buyer's real estate broker will assist in preparing the board packet. The broker should insure that all the necessary material is gathered and complete, and should submit the completed documentation to the managing agent. Usually, the board will not schedule an interview until after the board packet, including all supporting documentation, has been deemed complete.

STEP 5
CLOSING THE TRANSACTION

After a buyer has been approved for a mortgage — and, in the case of a coop, has received approval from the board — the closing will take place. The following people will normally be present: you and your attorney; the seller and his or her attorney; a representative for the bank providing you with a loan; a bank representative for the loan being paid off by the seller; the managing agent representing the building; and the real estate broker. If the purchase is a condominium, there will usually also be a representative from a title insurance company who will verify and insure that clear title is being transferred by the seller.

During the closing, you will sign the documents required by the bank to issue your loan. The bank will give the loan proceeds to your attorney on your behalf, and your attorney will then give them to the seller's attorney. In addition, you will be requested to provide a certified check, made payable to the seller, for the difference between the loan proceeds, the initial 10% deposit, and the full purchase price. You also will be asked to make a payment for that portion of building maintenance (or common charge in the case of a condominium) allocated for the remainder of the month. In the case of a cooperative, the stock and lease associated with the apartment will be given to the bank to hold as its collateral. In a last act, you will be handed the keys to your apartment. Congratulations!

COOP CLOSING COSTS

THE BUYER

ESTIMATED COSTS

Appraisal Fee:	$ 450
Credit Report Fee:	$ 75
Mortgage Points —	
1% – 2% of Loan (if any):	$1,000 → (based on $100,000 loan)
"Mansion Tax" for sales of $1M+:	? → 1% of the sale price
Bank Underwriting Fee:	$ 350
Bank Legal Fees:	$ 600
UCC Lien Search:	$ 250
UCC Filing Fee:	$ 25
Coop Board Application:	$ 500
Coop Credit Report:	$ 75
Buyer's Attorney:	$1,500 (approximate)
Move-in Deposit:	$1,000 → refundable in most cases
Move-in Fee:	$ 250
Prepaid Expenses:	? → mortgage and maintenance to the end of the month

COOP CLOSING COSTS

THE SELLER

ESTIMATED COSTS

NY City Transfer Tax: $25 filing fee plus…

    For sales under $500K: 1% of the sale price

    For sales over $500K: 1.425% of the sale price

NY State Transfer Tax: .4% (.004) of the sale price

Seller's Attorney: $1,500 (approximate)

Coop Flip Tax (if any):   varies; can be calculated as a percent of the sale price or the profit, or a cost per share

Managing Agent Fee: $450 → processing fees

Move-out Deposit: $1,000 → refundable in most cases

Move-out Fee: $500

Bank Fees (if any): $250 → processing fees for mortgage payoff

CONDOMINIUM CLOSING COSTS

THE BUYER

ESTIMATED COSTS

Appraisal Fee:	$ 450	
Credit Report Fee:	$ 75	
Mortgage Points — (1% – 2% of Loan, if any):	$1,000 →	(based on $100,000 loan)
Bank Underwriting Fee:	$ 350	
Bank Legal Fees:	$ 600	
Mortgage Tax:	$1,750 →	1.75% under $500K; 2.125% over $500K
Title Search:	$ 500 →	(based on $100,000 loan)
"Mansion Tax" for sales of $1M+:	? →	1% of the sale price
Title Insurance:	$ 700 →	(based on $100,000 loan)
Recording Charge:	$ 200	
Buyer's Attorney:	$1,500	(approximate)
Condo Board Application:	$ 500	
Condo Credit Report:	$ 75	
Prepaid Expenses:	? →	mortgage and common charges to the end of the month; real estate tax escrow up to six months
Move-in Deposit:	$1,000 →	refundable upon completion of move
Move-in Fee:	$ 250	

CONDOMINIUM CLOSING COSTS

THE SELLER

ESTIMATED COSTS

NY City Transfer Tax:	$ 25 filing fee plus…
For sales under $500K:	1% of the sale price
For sales over $500K:	1.425% of the sale price
NY State Transfer Tax:	.4% (.004) of the sale price
Seller's Attorney:	$ 1,500 (approximate)
Managing Agent Fee:	$ 450 → processing fees
Move-out Deposit:	$ 1,000 → refundable in most cases
Move-out Fee:	$ 500
Bank Fees (if any):	$ 500 → processing fees for mortgage payoff

The Forms of Home Ownership and Occupancy

COOPERATIVE OWNERSHIP

Definition:

A cooperative is a corporation that owns a building. Each apartment is allocated a number of shares of stock, the sum of which equals all the shares outstanding of the corporation. These shares of stock are the evidence of ownership. In addition to the shares, each apartment receives a proprietary lease, which affirms the owner's right to occupy a specific apartment. "Tenant-Shareholders" pay a monthly charge, called maintenance, which covers their allocable portion of the costs of operating the building, the building's real estate taxes and the debt service on the building's mortgage (generally referred to as the "underlying mortgage"). Coop owners are entitled to a tax deduction for their portion of the building's real estate tax and their portion of the building's interest payment on its mortgage. They are also entitled to deduct the interest payment on their own apartment loan.

Generally:

Cooperative corporations began as social clubs and as a means of restricting who could move into a building. This form of ownership grew in popularity in the 1960s, 70s, and 80s, however, not because of any exclusionary impulse but as a result of restrictive rent laws existing in the City at that time. Though operating costs were rising dramatically due to inflation and exploding fuel costs, government limits on rent increases to tenants made it impossible for landlords to cover the increasing cost of operating their buildings. Conversion to coop ownership became a way to escape this burden. The cooperative form was preferred for the following reasons:

• The New York State law regulating the conversion of apartment buildings to cooperative ownership (the Martin Act, Section 352, New York General Business Law, including added regulations) was relatively clear and had worked effectively in New York over the years.

•Coop conversions did not usually necessitate repayment of existing low interest rate building mortgages. When coop conversions were at their peak, banks were resistant to issuing new mortgages and charged extremely high interest rates on such loans when they did. However, many existing mortgages had no restrictions on converting a building to cooperative ownership so the existing loans could be maintained on the property. This proved enticing to landlords because it permitted them to cash out of their economic predicament and at the same time offer a marketable product at a low monthly cost to the owner.

•Coops were qualified to pass through to the individual tenant-stockholders the same federal and state tax deductions available for other forms of home ownership (with some limitations).

•A bandwagon effect took place. Successful coop conversions inspired emulation, which created a trend.

ADVANTAGES OF COOPERATIVE OWNERSHIP

1. **Tax deductibility:** The owner is entitled to a tax deduction for real estate taxes and mortgage interest under federal and state law.

2. **Board approval:** A coop will normally require any prospective owner to go through an approval process as a condition of ownership. This insures that the owner meets certain standards which the board of directors, as representatives of the apartment owners in the building, feel are appropriate to becoming an owner. It allows the board to determine if potential new members of the coop are financially capable of supporting their home and

carrying their share of the building's expenses. It also allows the board to screen out those who would not make desirable neighbors (subject to federal, state and local discrimination laws).

3. Popularity: Approximately 75% of all apartments owned in New York City are in the form of cooperative ownership. Therefore, this form of apartment ownership offers a buyer the greatest selection of buildings to choose from.

DISADVANTAGES OF COOPERATIVE OWNERSHIP

1. Limitations of tax deductibility under certain circumstances: There are legal criteria a cooperative must meet to qualify for state and federal tax advantages. If a building fails to meet these criteria, apartment owners will not be permitted to take the tax deductions otherwise normally allowed. This restriction doesn't exist in other forms of home ownership.

2. Board approval process: The approval process requires disclosure of significant personal and financial information which some prospective buyers prefer not to disclose. The process also makes the purchase more uncertain, since its successful conclusion is contingent on board approval.

3. Limited right to rent: Though most cooperative corporations do allow owners the right to rent under limited circumstances and for a limited duration, it is often a cumbersome procedure, which requires prospective tenants to go through an approval process prior to taking occupancy. Therefore, renting a coop apartment is usually more difficult than renting a condo or single family home. In addition, cooperative corporations often charge a sublet fee, which varies in amount but can be material.

4. Higher interest rate on home loans: The rate of interest on a coop apartment loan is generally higher than the rate offered for a condominium or a house by approximately 0.5%.

5. Equity requirement: While condominiums allow buyers to finance up to 90% of their purchase, coop boards rarely permit this. Financing is commonly limited to 75% of the purchase price, and in many cooperative buildings this limitation is even more restrictive. Indeed, some buildings require all equity cash purchases.

CONDOMINIUMS

Definition:

A Condominium is an apartment building in which each apartment owner has a percentage of the ownership of the entire property, and each owner receives a unit deed evidencing that ownership. Each condo owner pays a "common charge," which is a monthly payment covering their share of the costs of operating the building. Real estate taxes are paid directly to the City by each individual apartment owner, and there is no underlying building mortgage. By legal definition, a condominium is considered real property, while a cooperative is considered personal property.

Generally:

Condominiums, as a form of home ownership, began in the 1960s when Congress passed legislation permitting the creation of Housing Associations as taxable entities. They first became popular in the South and West, where large amounts of new housing were being created. Condominiums offer a means to maintain common property and provide common amenities within the framework of common ownership.

Condominiums became a force in the New York City market in the early 1980s. At that time, there was tremendous upward pressure on interest rates. Banks were literally paying more to borrow money than they were receiving as income on some of their long-term outstanding loans. In order for the banks to protect themselves, they were only willing to offer borrowers short-term loans with variable interest rates. While this reduced the banks' level of risk, it created difficulties for developers seeking long-term mortgage financing for their newly-developed properties.

Banks, therefore, proposed "end loan unit financing." In this framework, the banks replaced the all-encompassing construction loan, initially issued to to build the building, with smaller mortgages, each associated with a condominium unit. To the banks, the condominium form was important, since these mortgages could easily be resold to brokerage firms on Wall Street, who in turn would create bulk packages to be sold on the financial markets. Developers were therefore compelled to choose the condominium form in order to obtain financing for their projects. Almost a decade would pass before the financial markets would offer similar outlets for coop loans.

ADVANTAGES OF CONDOMINIUM OWNERSHIP

1. Right to rent: In contrast to the restrictions on renting commonly found in cooperatives, there is no, or a limited, approval process required in a condominium. When there is a requirement for approval, it is normally in the form of a "Right of First Refusal." This permits the board to reject a proposed renter, but obligates it to rent the apartment under the same terms and conditions expressed in a bona fide lease agreement. The board cannot turn down a renter and leave the owner with no alternatives, as in a coop.

2. Flexibility in purchase: Normally, the sale of a condominium unit does not require the elaborate review process found in most cooperatives. However, many condos do require a "Right of First Refusal" review. This permits the condo association the right to purchase the apartment on the same terms and conditions offered to the purchaser in a consummated contract of sale. Where there is a Right of First Refusal provision in the condominium bylaws, a prospective purchaser may have to submit personal information, including financial data, for the completion of this review process. From the seller's point of view, there is a sale in any event. The condominium right is merely to step into the shoes of the buyer, not to reject the transaction outright. Accordingly, the certainty of completing the sale after the contract has been consummated is greater in a condo than in a coop.

3. Lower interest rates: The rate of interest charged by banks for a condo mortgage is approximately 0.5% less than the rate charged for a coop apartment loan.

4. No equity requirement: A purchaser is not restricted in the amount of debt he or she can use to finance the apartment. Normally, coops require a minimum of 25% equity capital.

5. Controllable financing: Because there is no building mortgage (just the individual condominium owner's mortgage) and real estate taxes are paid directly to the City by the apartment owner, common charges consist of operating costs only. Therefore, if an owner is seeking to pay "all equity cash" for an apartment, the monthly cost of ownership in a condominium can be lower than it would be in a comparable cooperative apartment, since there is no debt service in the monthly payment to cover the building's underlying mortgage.

DISADVANTAGES OF CONDOMINIUM OWNERSHIP

1. Transience: It is relatively easy to rent out a condominium apartment. As a result, more people move in and out of the building. A high level of turnover can diminish the sense of community and there may be more wear and tear on the building's common areas.

2. Control: Since the board approval process in a condominium is usually limited, it is much harder to place restrictions on who moves in. When people with marginal finances fail to pay common charges, the cost of unpaid maintenance must be borne by the other homeowners. In addition, when an owner's behavior is disruptive, the condominium must seek to legally enjoin the behavior or initiate a foreclosure procedure, which must be based on a violation of the unit deed. In a cooperative, alternatives such as eviction are available via the proprietary lease. Foreclosure in a condominium can be much more costly and time-consuming.

3. Transaction costs: The closing costs for a condominium are somewhat higher than with a cooperative. This is due in large part to mortgage recording costs and title insurance, which are not applicable to coops.

4. "Lien risk": When purchasing a condo, the buyer is obtaining a mortgage on real property. If the common charges are unpaid, this obligation becomes a "subordinate lien" to the recorded first mortgage and to any unpaid real estate taxes. This effectively means that the condo association is last in line with respect to repayment of its unpaid common charges. In the event of foreclosure, the condo association runs the risk that proceeds received will not be enough to cover the first mortgage, the unpaid real estate taxes, and the legal fees incurred in the foreclosure process. In such a case, the condo's claim can be effectively "wiped out," and the association will never be reimbursed for payments made on behalf of the delinquent unit owner.

This is not the case with a coop. The coop buyer is obtaining a "financing" secured by shares of stock, not by real estate. Appurtenant to the stock is a proprietary lease. In the event that a coop owner fails to pay the maintenance, the claim of the cooperative corporation can continue since it correlates to the lease on the property as distinguished from the property itself. Any action of foreclosure on the stock does not adversely affect the cooperative corporation's rights under the proprietary lease.

In a nutshell, a cooperative corporation's right to make a claim for unpaid monthly charges takes precedence over the rights of a lending bank. In a condominium it's the other way around; the condo association's right to monthly charges is subordinate to the bank.

TENANCY IN COMMON

Definition:
A tenancy in common is an agreement in which each apartment owner has a proportionate ownership of the total building and exclusive use of a specific apartment. Each owner pays maintenance to cover the operating costs, real estate taxes, and any mortgage on the entire building. There is no stock or proprietary lease, and there is no unit deed. The legal rights of the owner are derived solely from the tenancy in common agreement.

ADVANTAGES OF A TENANCY IN COMMON

1. Informality: Buildings owned under a tenancy in common agreement are usually small. This helps to create a sense of informality and flexibility in solving building problems. In contrast, cooperatives and condominiums have larger and more formalized organizational structures, which usually means that decisions take longer.

2. Formation cost: The legal fees required to form a tenancy in common are less than those required to form a condominium or cooperative.

3. Sense of community: In a tenancy in common building, everyone contributes for the common good. All the affairs of the building are addressed and resolved by all the owners together.

DISADVANTAGES OF A TENANCY IN COMMON

1. Informality: Informality in managing the building can lead to misunderstandings and disputes which can seriously affect the building's operation and condition.

2. Lack of professional management: Many tenancy in common buildings are self-managed, which means that the maintenance of the building — including basic functional duties — are the responsibility of the owners, not a professional management company or building staff.

3. Lack of market: Only a small number of buildings are structured as tenancies in common because acceptance of this as a form of home ownership has been limited. This lack of popularity can significantly reduce the resale value of the property unless the entire building is sold at one time.

4. Lack of financing: It is very difficult for a buyer of an apartment under a tenancy in common agreement to get financing from a bank. Financing must normally be offered by the seller, or the apartment must be purchased "all equity cash."

5. Liability: As a result of the joint ownership, actions taken by one member create obligations for all the owners. This could lead to misunderstandings when one owner makes commitments inconsistent with the wishes of others. Each owner can be legally responsible for the full amount of any obligations incurred.

SINGLE FAMILY PROPERTY

Definition:
A single family dwelling is a building for which the owner has the deed to the property and is solely responsible for all costs and maintenance of the entire property.

ADVANTAGES OF A SINGLE FAMILY PROPERTY

1. Controllable environment: The costs associated with running the property are solely the responsibility of the owner, and there can be no assessment or other cost levied by a vote of a board of directors.

2. Discretionary use: The use of the property is not subject to rules and conditions set by a board or other external authority other than local zoning ordinances.

3. Space: Usually, single family properties offer more interior space, as well as amenities not frequently found in cooperative or condominium apartments, such as backyards.

4. Privacy: Single family homeowners don't have to share private information, such as their financial affairs, with their neighbors. And if they wish to make alterations to their property, they don't have to ask a board of directors for permission.

DISADVANTAGES OF A SINGLE FAMILY PROPERTY

1. Security: There is less control over who enters the premises of a single family property than there is in cooperative and condominium buildings. Coops and condos usually have employees in regular attendance or other common-area security measures which are not always possible for a single family property.

2. Maintenance: The duty of overseeing the property rests fully on the owner. There is no manager or staff to insure that the physical plant is maintained in good working order, and no neighbors to help share the burden.

3. Cost: Purchasing a single family home, particularly in Manhattan, is cost-prohibitive for many people.

4. Real estate taxes: In condominiums and cooperatives, the real estate assessed value is determined at the building level, and there is no change in the assessment of real estate taxes when an apartment changes hands. However, in a single dwelling property, the sale price of the property could result in a reassessment of the taxable value, which in turn could increase the yearly tax liability.

RENTAL PROPERTY

Definition:
Rental property is a form of occupancy rather than ownership. There is a lease which prescribes the occupant's use and possession of the property, under defined terms and for a limited duration. There are few of the risks or rewards associated with ownership.

ADVANTAGES OF A RENTAL PROPERTY

1. No risk of ownership: The increase or decrease in real estate values is not an issue for renters, since they have no money at risk.

2. Limited duration: Renters can limit the length of time they wish to stay in a property without worrying about selling it upon leaving.

3. Broader service: Usually, more services are expected by a tenant in a rental property than by a unit owner. For example, in a rental, if appliances are in need of repair or the walls need to be painted, the landlord is usually responsible, while in a cooperative or condominium these are the responsibility of the apartment owner.

4. Liquidity: The renter's financial assets remain available for an alternative investment, which may have a higher economic return than owning a home.

DISADVANTAGES OF A RENTAL PROPERTY

1. No economic gain: Real estate, over the long term, has usually proved to be an excellent investment, offering attractive economic returns and favorable tax treatment when the property is sold. This tax benefit is not available to renters.

2. No tax advantages: The tax deductibility of interest and real estate taxes frequently make it cheaper to own than to rent.

3. Aesthetic: Renters are usually reluctant to make significant improvements in their apartments since they know their investment won't bring them any financial return. Indeed, many landlords prohibit alterations of the property. Therefore, it is not easy to customize rental property to fit the lifestyle of the tenant.

4. No permanence: A renter is subject to the terms of a lease, which includes limits on the duration of his or her occupancy. The tenant may have to move at the end of the lease term.

Evaluating the "Rent vs. Buy" Alternative

Understanding the costs of renting vs. ownership is an important beginning point in deciding which choice to make. However, choosing to rent or buy is not just an economic decision. There are a number of other important factors that must be evaluated.

ISSUE 1
PERMANENCE

There are people who are reluctant to make a long-term commitment to a specific apartment or geographic area.

According to Bellmarc records, the average length of time a homeowner stays in a Manhattan apartment is five years. People living in large apartments, particularly if they have children in school, stay somewhat longer. People in smaller apartments, particularly if they are young and single, tend to stay for a shorter term.

Think of a young person moving into his or her first owned home; it's probably a studio. Before long, salary increases allow a move to a larger apartment, possibly a one bedroom. Then, with marriage and two incomes,

comes a nicer one bedroom apartment, or a two bedroom becomes a viable alternative. Within a few years, children arrive and the young couple feel pressured to move to an even larger home. This whole process frequently happens within a period of ten years!

Permanence is a state of mind with most buyers. Very few actually stay in their apartments for the long term. Rather, the home they buy is merely the right apartment for the moment, until a better opportunity or a change in lifestyle warrants a new alternative.

ISSUE 2
FEAR

The responsibility of home ownership and the magnitude of the decision can be intimidating, especially to those with no prior experience or with a negative experience.

Fear is a legitimate reason for not buying an apartment, especially considering the size of the investment and the potential risks. Almost everyone experiences some degree of anxiety when faced with the prospect of buying a home. Usually, however, lack of knowledge is what precipitates the fear and uncertainty.

Acquiring even a bit of knowledge about the advantages and disadvantages of home ownership can make you feel a lot more confident that you are making a wise decision. One useful idea is to perform a full "rent vs. buy" analysis (see page 46). This will enable you to better understand the economic consequences of each alternative. Whatever your decision, doing a rent vs. buy analysis will help you know that your options have been carefully and logically considered.

One mistake some buyers make is to seek a "needle-in-the-haystack" apartment that outshines all others. These buyers view literally hundreds of properties without making any offers. It is as if they are afraid to commit themselves because they believe that the "special one" is just around the corner. If you find yourself in this position, I propose that it would be wise to take a second look at apartments that you previously rejected. Consider whether there is a lower price, even if that price is substantially lower, where the apartment could meet your needs. If so, put in a low offer. Sometimes these bids end up in great deals. However, think about justifying your offer. Create an appropriate reason why your bid is a reasonable figure for the seller to consider.

A good exercise is to mentally create the apartment you desire and determine a price you would be willing to pay for it. Then, look in the newspaper. Is that price consistent with prices asked for comparable properties? Ask a broker if the apartment and price you are seeking is achievable. If the broker says no, ask him or her to give you supporting information. It is essential to be informed. Knowledge of the market will give you the confidence to put in bids in order to take advantage of opportunities.

ISSUE 3
ECONOMIC TRENDS

The risks and returns of buying a home may be viewed as less than ideal in light of current economic trends.

I recall reading a newspaper article predicting that the real estate bubble was about to burst. The writer noted that prices were ridiculously high, and that any day the entire market would collapse. The writer was Alexander Hamilton; the era was the late 1700s and homes were selling for about $100.

Perceptions of inflated real estate values are nothing new. However, I would place my bet that real estate values will continue to increase. Consider this: according to bank rules for mortgage lending, up to 40% of your income can be applied to the cost of carrying a home. Therefore, for each dollar your salary increases, your ability to carry a loan increases by about forty cents. However, this is the *cost* to carry the loan, not the principal amount. The principal is determined by dividing this extra money by the available interest rate. For example, if the rate is 10%, this additional forty cents can support an additional loan amount of $4.00. Simply stated, for every dollar your income goes up you can afford to borrow four dollars more. Do you know anyone who would be happy next year without an increase in their income? I don't. More income equals more mortgage, which in turn equals higher values.

Add to this a declining supply. That's right, declining! The number of new apartments currently being built in New York City is insufficient to replace the depleting housing stock of obsolete apartments. New York is experiencing a net reduction in dwelling units each year.

The conclusion to be drawn is rather clear. Even if everything stayed the same and supply and demand were in balance, the effect of inflation would naturally increase prices due to the leveraging effect of borrowing. However, supply is not keeping up with demand, and incomes are rising dramatically so the impact on prices is even more significant.

There is no question that real estate values go through economic cycles. However, after every single decline, prices have risen to more than they were at the high point of the prior cycle. Few investments have as good a long-term track record.

ISSUE 4
LIFE OBJECTIVES

Buying a home may be viewed as inconsistent with one's current life objectives.

Everyone has their own set of priorities. It's not surprising that some people don't look upon home ownership as one of their life objectives. The following are some key points these people should consider:

• A home is the epitome of security. It is the one place where you can feel safe from outside pressures and influences. In terms of personal growth and development, homeownership is frequently considered the "next step."

• For most people, a home is the best financial investment they will ever make, one which will provide their greatest source of wealth accumulation.

• Many banks prefer to lend to homeowners rather than renters, because the real estate they own represents a significant and tangible asset which is valuable security. Presently, accounting rules require that the value of your home be listed on your personal financial statement at its current fair market value rather than its initial cost. This means that your home is accumulating tangible wealth in the form of increased creditworthiness without your having to sell it.

Home ownership provides many benefits beyond the obvious. If you believe home ownership is inconsistent with your life objectives, it is probably because you are not looking at all the possible opportunities owning a cooperative or condominium apartment can offer.

ISSUE 5
LIQUIDITY

To some people, liquidity is like an insurance policy against the effects of future uncertainty. Using one's available cash to buy a home may eliminate this protection.

There is no question that if you use your money to purchase a home you have made a commitment that cannot be quickly altered. If the funds you are thinking about investing in real estate are essential to maintaining your lifestyle, you should think twice. On the other hand, purchasing a home is often the first step toward creating wealth. You build equity both through your home's appreciation and through yearly tax savings.

You can also use your home to get cash by means of an equity credit line. This is a bank line of credit which uses the appreciation you built up in your home as security for the loan. Funds can be borrowed and paid back at will, and interest is only charged on the balance outstanding. The rate of interest on an equity credit line is normally very attractive, and the interest charge is tax deductible as homeowner interest as long as the borrowed principal amount does not exceed $100,000. An equity credit line allows you to tap into the accumulated wealth in your home as and when funds are needed. Equity credit lines are available from most major banks or from mortgage brokers at no (or minimal) cost.

USING THE RENT VS. BUY ANALYSIS CHARTS

This section is designed to help you evaluate the economic advantages and disadvantages of ownership and renting. There are two parts to this analysis: determining the cost of carrying a home, and comparing the returns on real estate to alternative investments. The following are the directions for using the worksheets that start on page 51.

PART 1
THE COST OF CARRYING A HOME

The question you will be answering is:
On a monthly after-tax basis, is it cheaper to rent an apartment or to own an apartment?

In order to answer this question, you must:

A. Select a prospective apartment to buy.

B. Select a prospective apartment to rent.

C. Determine the tax rate applicable to your highest-earned dollar by combining the federal rate with the New York State and New York City rates. A table of rates begins on page 152. Make sure to adjust your New York State and City rate by your federal rate, since state and local taxes are deductible on your federal tax return. To do this, multiply your state rate by (1.00 minus your federal rate). For example, if your income is $200,000 and you are married filing jointly, you are in the 36% federal tax bracket and the 10.6776% state and local tax bracket. This would compute to an after tax state and local rate of 6.833% (This figure was computed by multiplying 10.6776% × (1.00 -.36) = 6.833%). Thus, you have a combined total rate of 42.833% (36% federal plus 6.833% state and local taxes after adjustment).

D. Find the maintenance charge on the apartment you have selected as a prospective purchase and determine the tax deductible portion. You should be able to obtain this figure easily by asking the broker or the seller. In the absence of specific information, brokers generally use 50% of the maintenance fee as an approximation of the deductible portion.

Procedure:

Step 1. On the worksheet on page 51, enter the amount charged for renting the prospective apartment in Section I (A).

Step 2. In Section II: Tax Liability, enter the full maintenance charge for the prospective purchased apartment on the first line, entitled Maintenance. Make sure you take the monthly amount and multiply it by 12 to come up with the annual sum. Then, put the percent associated with the tax deductible portion (consisting of the real estate tax and building mortgage interest as a percent of the gross maintenance payment) in the second column. Finally, multiply the yearly maintenance charge (gross amount) by the tax deductible percent to compute the Yearly Tax Deductible Amount (last column).

Step 3. Multiply the proposed purchase price of the apartment by 75% (.75). This is the assumed amount to be financed. Then, go to page 116 and find the Debt Service Payment Table. Select the interest rate factor that you think would be applicable to your loan and identify the yearly payment per $1,000 of loan. This yearly payment consists of the interest charge on the funds borrowed as well as the principal repayment based on a 30-year amortization schedule.

Multiply the yearly payment per $1,000 of loan by the mortgage amount you calculated above (75% of the purchase price). This figure is your yearly loan payment, and should be entered on the second line, titled Debt Payment, in the first column.

To determine the tax deductible interest amount, multiply the financed amount by the pure interest rate (the interest rate excluding any principal amortization). The product of this calculation is the figure to place in the third column of the Debt Payment line, the Tax Deductible Amount. For example, if you borrow $300,000 at 10%, your annual tax deductible interest payment would be $30,000.

Step 4. Total the figures in the Gross Amount column (B). Then total the figures in the Tax Deductible Amount column.

Step 5. Add the Federal Tax Rate (page 152) and the State and City Tax rates (page 153) adjusted for federal taxes (see page 46, C), to determine the Total Tax Rate. Multiply the Total Tax Deductible Amount by the Total Tax Rate to arrive at your Computed Tax Effect (C). The Computed Tax Effect is the cash value of the tax deduction you received from ownership of the purchased property.

Step 6. Subtract (C), the Computed Tax Effect, from (B), the Total Gross Payment, to determine (D), the After-Tax Ownership Cost. Divide (D) by 12 to determine (E), the After-Tax Monthly Cost.

Step 7. Compare (A), the Applicable Rent for the Apartment, with (E), the Monthly Cost After Tax of Ownership. The difference between the two figures is (F), the Difference, Rent vs. Ownership: Monthly Cost. If (F) is a positive number (i.e., the rental number is higher than the ownership figure), then ownership will cost you less each month than renting.

PART 2
EVALUATING ALTERNATIVE INVESTMENTS

If you buy real estate, the return on your investment is a function of the appreciation of your property. If you do not buy real estate, your equity is available for some other investment opportunity. This section will show you how to evaluate the relative returns for each investment, so that you can decide which is the best alternative.

The question you will be answering is:
Which gives me a better return — the appreciation on a home or an alternate investment?

In order to answer this question, use the worksheet provided on page 52 and follow these instructions:
A. Identify an Alternate Investment, one in which you would place your

funds if you decided not to purchase a home. For comparative purposes, assume the amount you would invest is the same amount you would use to purchase a home — 25% of the purchase price.

B. Estimate the Investment Yield, which is the rate of return, you expect on this alternative investment in the foreseeable future.

C. Estimate the Rate of Inflation/Appreciation you expect for residential real estate in New York City. To do this, you can consider the prior year's rate of return, or you can ask real estate brokers, mortgage brokers, or others whose opinion you respect, what they anticipate. You can also use the level of increase in the local Consumer Price Index (CPI) if you believe prices will not increase beyond the level of inflation.

Procedure:
Step 1. In Section I: Investment, enter the amount you would invest in your alternative investment (25% of the purchase price) on the first line, titled Invested Funds.

Step 2. Enter the estimated Investment Yield on the second line.

Step 3. Compute your Yearly Investment Return (Line 3) by multiplying your invested funds by your Investment Yield.

Step 4. Apply your Total Tax Rate, determined in Part I (Step 5), to the yearly investment return (Line 3) to determine your Tax On Investment Income (Line 4). Subtract this amount from the Yearly Investment Return (Line 3) to determine your investment's Net After Tax Return (A).

Step 5. In Section II: Home Ownership, enter the Purchase Price of Home on the first line.

Step 6. On the second line, enter the Rate of Inflation/Appreciation you estimate to be applicable to your home.

Step 7. Multiply the Purchase Price of Home (Line 1) by the Inflation/

Appreciation rate (Line 2) to determine the Yearly Appreciation Benefit, After Tax (B). This number is already an after-tax figure, because the profit from the sale of a home is free from tax on the first $250,000 for a single person ($500,000 for a couple). For amounts in excess of these figures the tax is at the capital gains rate of 20%.

Step 8. Subtract (A) from (B) to determine the Relative Yearly Benefit of Investment to Home Ownership.

In evaluating investment returns, remember that home ownership has the advantage of substantial leverage, which is effectively interest-free since the interest cost has already been considered in determining the relative monthly cost of owning vs. renting.

RENT VS. BUY ANALYSIS

PART 1

ANALYSIS OF MONTHLY EFFECT

SECTION I: RENT ALTERNATIVE

The Applicable Rent for the Apartment $_____ **(A)**

SECTION II: TAX LIABILITY

DESCRIPTION OF PAYMENT	GROSS AMOUNT (ANNUAL)	PERCENT DEDUCTIBLE	TAX DEDUCTIBLE AMOUNT
Maintenance	$_____	_____%	$_____
Debt Payment	$_____	Interest Portion: $_____	
Total	$_____ **(B)**		$_____

Federal Tax Rate _____% + State & Local Tax Rate* _____%

= Total Tax Rate _____%

Computed Tax Effect $_____ **(C)**

SECTION III: RENT VS. BUY COMPARISON

After Tax Ownership Cost, (B) − (C) $_____ **(D)**

Monthly Cost, After Tax (D divided by 12) $_____ **(E)**

Rent vs. Ownership:
Monthly Cost (A) − (E) $_____ **(F)**

Therefore_____

_____

* Net of federal tax effect

RENT VS. BUY ANALYSIS

PART 2
ANALYSIS OF INVESTMENT RETURN

SECTION I: INVESTMENT

Invested Funds $_____

Investment Yield   _____ %

Yearly Investment Return $_____

Tax on Investment Income (Rate _____%) $_____

Net After Tax Return $_____ **(A)**

SECTION II: HOME OWNERSHIP

Purchase Price of Home $_____

Rate of Inflation/Appreciation   _____ %

Yearly Appreciation Benefit, After Tax* $_____ **(B)**

Relative Yearly Benefit (A) − (B) $_____

** In the event of a sale, the proceeds will be tax-free because current tax laws exempt
up to $250,000 in profit from taxation for individuals, or $500,000 per couple.*

Therefore_____

_____

EXAMPLE OF RENT VS. BUY

John Evans is considering renting an apartment for $2,500 per month. He is also evaluating buying a similar apartment for $300,000 with a monthly maintenance charge of $1,000. The broker has advised Mr. Evans that the tax deductible portion of the maintenance is 60%, and that financing is currently obtainable at 9% interest for 75% of the purchase price ($225,000).

In looking at page 116, John determines that the monthly payment rate per thousand is $8.05, or $96.60 per thousand per year. John can take the principal sum he would borrow, $225,000, and multiply it by .0966 to get the yearly payment required to carry the proposed mortgage, $21,735. To determine the interest portion of his yearly payment, John takes the amount of the loan, $225,000, and multiplies it by the pure interest rate, 9%, to get $20,250.

John, who is married, earns $150,000 per year. Using the tables on pages 152 and 153, he determines that his federal tax rate is 31% for the upper portion of his income, and his state and local tax rate is 10.6776%. State and local taxes are deductible on his federal return, so his net tax rate for state and local taxes is actually 7.3675%. This is computed by taking the state and local tax rate and multiplying it by 1.00 minus the federal rate. In this example, 10.6776% × (1.00 - .31) = 7.3675%. John's total tax rate is 38.8675% (federal plus state and local tax rates).

If John does not purchase a home but decides to rent, he will take his savings and place it into an alternative investment that gives a yield of 6%. He believes that real estate values will increase by 3% per year.

John has the $75,000 down payment in cash to invest in the apartment. In light of this information, he performs the following analysis:

RENT VS. BUY ANALYSIS

PART 1

ANALYSIS OF MONTHLY EFFECT
(All numbers are rounded to the nearest dollar)

SECTION I: RENT ALTERNATIVE

The Applicable Rent for the Apartment $_____$2,500_____ **(A)**

SECTION II: TAX LIABILITY

DESCRIPTION OF PAYMENT	GROSS AMOUNT (ANNUAL)	PERCENT DEDUCTIBLE	TAX DEDUCTIBLE AMOUNT
Maintenance	$____12,000[1]____	60 %	$____7,200____
Debt Payment	$____21,735[2]____	Interest Portion:	$____20,250____
Total	$____33,735____ **(B)**		$____27,450____

Federal Tax Rate ____31____% + State & Local Tax Rate __7.3675[3]__ %

= Total Tax Rate ____38.3675__ %

Computed Tax Effect $____10,532____ **(C)**

SECTION III: RENT VS. BUY COMPARISON

After Tax Ownership Cost (B) – (C) $____23,203____ **(D)**

Monthly Cost After Tax (D divided by 12) $____1,933____ **(E)**

Rent vs. Ownership:
Monthly Cost (A) – (E) $____567____ **(F)**

Therefore _owning the apartment is a more favorable financial alternative, by_

$567 per month, than renting the apartment.

[1] Monthly maintenance = $1,000 x 12 months = $12,000 gross annual amount.
[2] Borrowed amount of $225,000 x debt payment rate of .0966 = $21,735
[3] Adjustment for net of federal tax is 10.6776% x (1.00 - .31) = 7.3675%

RENT VS. BUY ANALYSIS

PART 2

ANALYSIS OF INVESTMENT RETURN

SECTION I: INVESTMENT

Invested Funds	$ 75,000	
Investment Yield	6 %	
Yearly Investment Return	$ 4,500	
Tax on Investment Income (Rate 38.3675 %)	$ 1,726	
Net After Tax Return	$ 2,774	**(A)**

SECTION II: HOME OWNERSHIP

Purchase Price of Home	$ 300,000	
Rate of Inflation/Appreciation	3 %	
Yearly Appreciation Benefit, After Tax*	$ 9,000	**(B)**
Relative Yearly Benefit (A) – (B)	$ 6,226	

* *In the event of a sale, the proceeds will be tax-free as a result of current tax laws which exempt up to $250,000 in profit from taxation for individuals, or $500,000 per couple.*

Therefore *given the assumed yield and appreciation rates, investing in a home has a superior economic return of $6,226 per year. This constitutes a higher return of over 224%, when compared to the alternative investment choice.*

The Science of Buying an Apartment

Purchasing an apartment is a major decision, so wouldn't it make sense to evaluate your options using a tested method? The following is one of the techniques Bellmarc salespeople are trained to use.

Every purchasing decision has an underlying buying formula. A recipe, if you will, composed of the critical components involved in the evaluation process. The first step in buying an apartment is to identify these criteria, and then to understand the relative importance of each one in your decision-making process. I have found several recurring qualities that buyers seem to care most about. They fall into two categories. The first category, referred to as the "Primary Motivators," relates to the specific location, the building and the air, light and space in the apartment. The second category encompasses economic factors, and relates to cash down payment and monthly cost. These are referred to as the "Financial Motivators."

UNDERSTANDING THE PRIMARY MOTIVATORS

It is important not merely to understand what you want in an apartment in a general sense, but also to create a means to evaluate various choices by specific criteria. These criteria should serve as benchmarks by which each choice is measured and prioritized against others.

Measuring the merits of your criteria allows you to create a buying formula. This is your delineated statement of what it is you would like to buy. Through experience, I have found that there are certain criteria, which I refer to as the "Primary Motivators," that are almost always important. The following is a definition of each Primary Motivator, as well as its recommended form of measurement. Use this information to help you fill out the worksheets for evaluating and comparing apartments on pages 66 to 73.

Location:
"Location" is the quality of the area in which a building is situated and includes aesthetic features, the quality and nature of local services, convenience to transportation, and reputation. A good way to understand the unique qualities of various neighborhoods is to review Bellmarc's Neighborhood Survey. Find it at the internet site **bellmarc.com**.
Form of measurement: Use a grade from "1" to "10" with "1" being the least desirable location and "10" being an optimal location.

Building:
"Building" is the aesthetics of the property, its condition, its amenities, its services, and its general reputation.
Form of measurement: Use a grade from "1" to "10" with "1" being a building that is undesirable and "10" being a building with optimal qualities.

Air:
"Air" is a term of art. It relates to the sense of openness, layout, and the level of "usability" of the apartment.
Form of Measurement: Describe the specific elements of Air, including layout features and the qualities of openness, that are relevant to your purchasing decision.

Light:
"Light" is also a term of art. It consists of two components: the height up from the street and the view.
Form of measurement: Light is measured by the apartment's floor and by

the predominant view from its prominent room, usually the living room. The view should be evaluated using a grade from "1" to "10." A grade of "1" represents a dark, unattractive view and a grade of "10" is a grand view with high aesthetic appeal.

Space:
"Space" is the size of the apartment.

Form of measurement: Space should not be evaluated just by square footage. Rather, it is important to consider how the space is effectively used. I have found it helpful to measure the dimensions of what I call the "Value Rooms," which I believe are the rooms that are most important to most buyers. The Value Rooms are the Living Room, Dining Area and Master Bedroom. The Dining Area (or room) is considered as an alternative use of the Living Room, so this space is combined with the Living Room dimension. The inclusion of only the measurements of the Value Rooms does not mean that other rooms, such as Second Bedrooms, Kitchens and the like, are not meaningful. Rather, the Value Rooms are critical areas in the apartment which must meet minimum thresholds in order for the apartment to be seriously considered as a whole.

IDENTIFYING THE FINANCIAL MOTIVATORS

In addition to aesthetic considerations, there are economic criteria that almost every buyer uses in making a decision. I refer to these as "Financial Motivators." Contrary to what many people believe, price is not the most important feature in evaluating the economics of buying an apartment. Rather, it is cost. This includes both the cash down payment and the monthly cost of carrying the home. While price and maintenance (or common charge and real estate taxes in the case of a condominium) is how brokers present and discuss properties, astute buyers quickly convert this into the number most meaningful to them: cash down and cash per month. The following is a definition for each Financial Motivator, as well as its recommended form of measurement, to be used in filling out the worksheets.

Cash Down Payment:

This is the non-borrowed cash used to purchase the apartment.

Form of measurement: The amount of cash a buyer uses to purchase an apartment varies depending on his or her resources, cooperative board rules and bank lending requirements. However, none of these factors initially matter when you are deciding between apartments. Rather, the important element is relative cost. To determine this, it is essential to create an "apples to apples" comparison, so that all apartments are hypothetically considered on equal terms. Therefore, I propose that you use a down payment percentage for comparative purposes of 25% for all apartments.

Some people have problems understanding the need to create this hypothetical down payment percentage. Consider an example of two apartments. In one, the price is $500,000 and the maintenance is $5,000 per month. In the other, the price is $1,000,000 and the maintenance is $500 per month. Which is the better deal? Obviously, you need to create a common ground for comparison in order to draw a conclusion.

Assuming 25% down, it is clear that the down payment on the lower-priced apartment is one-half as much as the higher-priced apartment: $125,000 vs. $250,000. However, in terms of the monthly cost (debt payment plus maintenance) the lower priced apartment costs $7,884 per month while the higher-priced apartment costs $6,267 (assuming 8.5% interest for the debt on both apartments — see page 116). The difference in monthly cost is $1,617, or $19,404 per year. If you divide that amount by the difference in cash down payment ($125,000), the net result is 15.5%. This is an excessive cost of funds in an environment in which banks are charging substantially lower rates to borrow money. Therefore, the higher-priced apartment is the better deal because *its cost is less.*

Cost Per Month:

The monthly cost of the apartment consists of the maintenance charge plus the monthly mortgage payment (or the carrying charge, real estate taxes and the mortgage payment for a condominium).

Form of measurement: As with the Cash Down Payment, the Monthly Carrying Cost must be defined in a way that allows an "apples to apples" comparison with other apartments. Therefore, the mortgage principal amount is presumed to be 75% of the purchase price of the apartment.

Figure out your monthly debt service payment by multiplying this principal by the interest rate factor (see page 116). If any of the apartments are condominiums, reduce the bank loan rate by .5% since banks generally offer lower interest rates for condos than for coops. (However, if you are considering using 90% heavy leverage to buy a condo, the rate between a condo and coop should be the same).

As a guideline, no more than 40% of your Gross Income should be used for carrying your home, and while banks will lend up to this percentage, it is higher than most coop boards will permit. Generally, their rule is closer to 30%.

THE STEP BY STEP PROCESS FOR CREATING A BUYING FORMULA

It would be useful to refer to the worksheets at the end of this chapter to best understand each step of this process. An example of applying the strategy is provided in the next chapter.

Step 1: Developing Parameters for Each Primary Motivator

The first step in buying a home is to develop a clear understanding of the meaning of each Primary Motivator by evaluating its component parts. You can do this by thinking about specific elements within each criteria and then evaluating the relative importance of each to you. For example, if you were to evaluate the Primary Motivator, Location, you might specifically consider the importance of tree-lined streets, the proximity to subways, or the residential/commercial mix of the area. Each one of these elements, and the others listed on the worksheet, should be rated for their degree of importance as you perceive it. At the conclusion, you should have a better perspective about what is the full meaning of that Primary Motivator to you.

In filling out the worksheets, grade each element on a scale of "1" to "10," using "1" when the element is unimportant and "10" when it is very important. Use the intervening grades "2, 3, 4, 5, 6, 7, 8, 9" as interim levels of desirability. Add any additional elements you can think of which matter to you in each category. I refer to this exercise as "Defining Your Parameters."

Step 2: Defining Your Range

Now that you have a clearer picture of the meaning of each Primary Motivator, you can draw conclusions that you can use in comparing specific apartments. What do you like? What do you not like? Create a statement of what would be ideal for you for each Primary Motivator and call it a "10." Create another statement of what the worst would be and call it a "1." Now, identify a middle point between the extremes, which is a "5." By identifying the extremes and the middle point for each primary motivator, you are "Defining the Range."

This evaluation will help you develop an awareness of your feelings, not only at the outer levels of the range but for the full spectrum.

Step 3: Defining Flexibility

The conclusions you drew in "Defining Your Range" will help give you a sense of the relative importance of each Primary Motivator in your buying process. Now you should be able to develop a sense of your flexibility. You are searching for the minimum grade or value that you could assign to an apartment for that Primary Motivator and still have it be a viable alternative. This minimum is best determined by assuming that all other Primary Motivators are at optimal levels.

Understanding your level of flexibility for each Primary Motivator will permit you to respond to a less-than-ideal apartment with knowledge about your own adaptability. It is unlikely that you will find an ideal apartment that has no points of objection. Rather, there is always some degree of give and take in coming to a final decision.

Step 4: Identifying Secondary Factors

So far, you have analyzed the basic elements of an apartment and your feelings about them. However, there may be other factors that still call out to you, like outdoor space or fireplaces. If so, these should be added to the buyer formula. However, these "Secondary Factors" should be considered only after the Primary Motivators have been rated. They are rarely integral to selecting an apartment, but become important after a desirable apartment has been found. You do not buy a terrace with an apartment; you buy an apartment with a terrace.

It is useful to identify the cost associated with each Secondary Factor.

Try to find an apartment with the extra feature and a similar apartment without it. Knowing how much the Secondary Factor will cost you may impact your evaluation process.

Step 5: Understanding Cash Down Payment

On the Buyer Formula Worksheet (page 72) you are asked to write down the Cash Equity you want to invest. Don't put down all the money you have. There are transaction costs, move-in costs and incidental charges that must be taken into account before you determine the amount available to invest in an apartment. In addition, many cooperative boards are hesitant to approve applicants that appear illiquid. You should maintain a cash balance (or cash equivalents) after your down payment of a minimum of 10% of the purchase price.

Once you have identified your down payment sum, determine the "Implied" Price you can afford based on the Bank Debt/Equity Rule by multiplying this amount by 4 (see Qualifying for a Mortgage — page 107).

Step 6: Understanding Cash Per Month

On your Buyer Formula Worksheet you are asked to fill in the amount you want to spend monthly. A bank would compute the maximum appropriate amount by multiplying your Gross Income by 40%, then dividing this amount by 12 (in the event that you have other debt, you may have to make additional adjustments. See Qualifying For A Mortgage — page 107). However, most cooperatives will limit your monthly carrying cost to no more than 30% of Gross Income, and I recommend that you use this figure when doing your computations.

Next, determine the "Implied" Mortgage amount you can borrow using the Bank Carry Cost Rule (see Qualifying for a Mortgage, page 107). Take the monthly amount computed above, subtract the estimated maintenance associated with the type of property you are considering, and then divide that sum by the monthly interest rate factor (see page 116).

You can estimate the maintenance by looking in the classified section of a local newspaper. I particularly recommend the real estate section of the Sunday *New York Times*. By looking at the maintenance charges on advertised apartments of the price and type you are considering, you should be able to estimate an average maintenance for that kind of apartment.

Remember to figure into your computation the difference between the rate of interest charged by banks for mortgages on condominiums and that charged for loans on cooperatives. For a conventional condominium loan (where the debt/equity ratio is 75% / 25%), the interest rate should be 0.5% less than for a cooperative loan. However, if the condominium is purchased with deep leverage (90% financing), the interest rates are substantially the same.

With information about the Implied Price and the Implied Mortgage that you can carry, you can understand the economic limitations of your search.

Step 7: Creating Your Buying Formula

Having evaluated the Primary Motivators and the Financial Motivators, you can now complete the Buyer Formula Worksheet. This worksheet is your initial statement about the kind of property you would like to buy and what you can afford, both in price and monthly maintenance. Now that you have this fundamental information, you can begin the process of considering alternative apartments.

SELECTING AN APARTMENT AND MAKING AN OFFER

Searching for Apartments:

The primary vehicle for advertising apartments in New York City is the classified section of *The New York Times*. If you are searching for a high-priced apartment, you should also look in the back section of *The New York Times Magazine*. In addition, check the internet sites of various brokers (Bellmarc's is **bellmarc.com**) to get an impression of market offerings in your price range. I suggest that you perform this review before you call a broker, in order to get an initial independent impression of values.

I advise scanning the ads using one Primary Motivator as your initial screening device. Select the motivator that is most important to you, which I refer to as your "Crucial Determinant." While scanning the ads, circle only those apartments that meet your minimum requirements for the Crucial

Determinant. Then, evaluate the apartments you circled to find the ones that best reflect your buyer formula. For each of these, identify potential problems. In most instances, the apartment listings will be broker advertisements. Call the brokers to make further inquiries.

Communicating with a Broker:

When you call a real estate broker, normally you will be asked your name and telephone number to insure that you are registered with the firm. You should then ask about the advertised apartment. If it sounds interesting, make an appointment to see it at the earliest possible time. If you delay, you may find that it has been sold by the time you get there. In addition, describe your buyer formula and ask the broker to recommend other possibilities. Ideally, you should see between three and five apartments when you go on an appointment to have some points of comparison.

Going Out on Showings:

When you visit an apartment, try to picture yourself living in it. Imagine you just bought it and are moving in. Where would you eat? Where would you sleep? How would you utilize the space? After you envision the environment, ask yourself, "Would I be happy here?" This is not a price issue; it is a lifestyle decision. If the apartment doesn't work for you then it doesn't matter what the price is; it is not a candidate.

If you consider the apartment viable, you should go through a checklist of its strengths and weaknesses using the criteria you defined in your buyer formula. In the course of your search, don't expect to find the perfect fit. Consider the possible variations within your degree of flexibility. For example, one apartment might have a better location than you specified in your buyer formula, but it might be slightly smaller than you desire. Consider all the pros and cons to find properties which best fit your overall needs. After seeing a number of apartments, several candidates should stand out as worthy of serious consideration.

Comparing Alternative Properties:

Take your list of candidates and create a concise worksheet to compare them (see Comparative Worksheet For Viable Apartments, page 73). If one or more is a condo, make sure that you adjust the rate of interest down by

0.5%. From this final analysis, you should select one apartment which is your best choice. This is the apartment on which you should bid.

Bidding on an Apartment:

The first step in making a bid is determining what the apartment is worth to you. That is not the seller's asking price, but your sense of its value based on your impression of the market, the degree to which it meets your needs, and your economic limitations. When you have a figure in mind, you should consider making a bid below the asking price in order to negotiate the most favorable terms.

I suggest that you ask the broker about the flexibility of the seller. Then, develop a justification for your offer which the broker can use to communicate the legitimacy of your proposal. If the seller responds with an unacceptable counteroffer, ask the broker to get the seller's justification. If the response is reasonable, increase your offer if you can afford to. If the seller is not reasonable, renew your search.

PRIMARY MOTIVATORS WORKSHEET
LOCATION

Location refers to the area in which the building is situated and includes aesthetics, services, transportation, and reputation measures, among others.

Define the Parameters: Grade the relative importance to your overall purchasing decision of each item below, "I" being undesirable, "10" being optimal. Intervening grades (2, 3, 4, 5, 6, 7, 8, 9) express an interim level of importance.

Tree-lined streets	_____	Restaurants and culture	_____
Proximity to subways	_____	Noise level	_____
Commercial/residential mix	_____	Single/couple/family mix	_____
Perceived reputation of area	_____	Shopping	_____
Historic ambiance of block	_____	Proximity to parks	_____
_____	_____	_____	_____

Define the Range: Utilizing these parameters, create a general statement expressing your overall position on location, "I" being undesirable, "10" being optimal.

A grade "I" location is:_____

_____

A grade "10" location is: _____

_____

A grade "5" location is: _____

_____

Define your Flexibility: How important is Location in the context of all your other criteria?

Assuming all other elements were optimal, I would not buy an apartment if the Location grade was below _____

PRIMARY MOTIVATORS WORKSHEET
BUILDING

Building refers to a specific property and includes its aesthetic qualities, condition, services, building-wide amenities and perceived reputation.

Define the Parameters: Grade the relative importance to your overall purchasing decision of each item below, "1" being undesirable, "10" being optimal. Intervening grades (2, 3, 4, 5, 6, 7, 8, 9) express an interim level of importance.

Perceived building reputation_____		Architectural detail	_____
Modern	_____	Prewar	_____
Garage in building	_____	Elevator	_____
Building condition	_____	Common outdoor space	_____
Hi-rise	_____	Pool/health club	_____
Concierge	_____	Doormen	_____
_____	_____	_____	_____

Define the Range: Utilizing these parameters, create a general statement expressing your overall position on Building, "1" being undesirable, "10" being optimal.

A grade "1" building is: _____

_____

A grade "10" building is: _____

_____

A grade "5" building is: _____

_____

Define your Flexibility: How important is the Building in the context of all your other criteria?

Assuming all other elements were optimal, I would not buy an apartment if the Building grade was below _____

PRIMARY MOTIVATORS WORKSHEET
AIR AND LAYOUT

Air and Layout relate to the sense of openness of the apartment and the organization of the rooms.

Define the Parameters: Grade the relative importance to your overall purchasing decision of each item below, "1" being undesirable, "10" being optimal. Intervening grades (2, 3, 4, 5, 6, 7, 8, 9) express an interim level of importance.

High ceilings	_____	Eat-in kitchen	_____
Separate dining room	_____	Entry foyer	_____
Maid's room	_____	_____	_____

Define the Range: Not applicable.

Define your Flexibility: How important are the Air and Layout in the context of your other criteria?

Assuming all other elements were optimal, I would not buy an apartment if the following elements of Air and Layout were missing: _____
_____
_____

PRIMARY MOTIVATORS WORKSHEET
LIGHT

Light consists of two elements: **floor height** and the **predominant view** (typically determined by the living room window).

Determine the lowest floor on which you would live: _____

Define the Parameters: Grade the relative importance to your overall purchasing decision of each item below, "1" being undesirable, "10" being optimal. Intervening grades (2, 3, 4, 5, 6, 7, 8, 9) express an interim level of importance.

Cityscape view	_____	Park view	_____
River view	_____	Local street view	_____
Commercial street view	_____	Building across street view	_____
Courtyard view	_____	Direct sun	_____
_____	_____	_____	_____

Define the Range: Utilizing these parameters, create a general statement expressing your overall position on Light, "1" being undesirable, "10" being optimal.

A grade "1" view is: _____

_____

A grade "10" view is: _____

_____

A grade "5" view is: _____

_____

Define your Flexibility: How important is the View in the context of all your other criteria?

Assuming all other elements were optimal, I would not buy an apartment if the View grade was below _____

PRIMARY MOTIVATORS WORKSHEET
SPACE

Space is not the total area in the apartment. Rather, it is the area contained in the "Value Rooms:" the Living Room, Dining Area and Master Bedroom.

Desired Living Room size   _____ x _____ = _____ sq. ft.

Desired Dining Area size (optional) _____ x _____ = _____ sq. ft.

Desired Master Bedroom size   _____ x _____ = _____ sq. ft.

Space of the Value Rooms   TOTAL = _____ sq. ft.

Define your Flexibility: How important is Space in the context of all your other criteria?

Assuming all other elements were optimal, I would not buy an apartment if the Space parameters were less than:

Living Room size   _____ x _____ = _____ sq. ft.

Dining Area size (optional) _____ x _____ = _____ sq. ft.

Master Bedroom size   _____ x _____ = _____ sq. ft.

PRIMARY MOTIVATORS WORKSHEET
SECONDARY FACTORS

Secondary factors are additional features which are not integral to the decision-making process unless the minimal requirements of Location, Building, Air and Layout, Light and Space have first been satisfied. These items do not need to be graded; simply check off or add other desired items.

Wood-burning fireplace   ( )   Terraces and outdoor space   ( )

_____   _____

_____   _____

BUYER FORMULA WORKSHEET
PRIMARY MOTIVATORS

Desired Location grade   _____   Desired Building grade   _____

Desired Air and Layout features _____

Desired Floor   _____   Desired View grade   _____

Space:

      Desired Living Room size   _____ × _____

      Desired Dining Room size (optional)   _____ × _____

      Desired Master Bedroom size   _____ × _____

Secondary Factors_____

_____

_____

FINANCIAL MOTIVATORS

Cash Down Payment $_____

Debt Equity Rule Multiplier   ×4

The Implied Price using Bank Debt/Equity Bank Rule $_____

Cost Per Month (30% of Gross Income divided by 12) $_____

Less: Estimated Maintenance Charge $_____

Available for Monthly Debt Payment $_____

Divide by: Debt Interest Factor *(see chart on page 116)*   _____ %

Implied Mortgage under Bank Carrying Cost Rule $_____

Add: Invested Cash Down Payment $_____

Implied Price using the Bank's 30% Carrying Cost Rule $_____

Price Range Guide $_____ to $_____

BUYER FORMULA WORKSHEET

COMPARATIVE WORKSHEET FOR VIABLE APARTMENTS

Address			
Location Grade	_____	_____	_____
Building Grade	_____	_____	_____
Air Qualities	_____	_____	_____
Light			
View Grade	_____	_____	_____
Floor	_____	_____	_____
Space			
Living Room	____ × ____	____ × ____	____ × ____
Dining Room	____ × ____	____ × ____	____ × ____
Master Bedroom	____ × ____	____ × ____	____ × ____
Secondary Factors	_____	_____	_____
Asking Price	$_____	$_____	$_____
Cash Down	$_____	$_____	$_____
Mortgage Amount	$_____	$_____	$_____

Applicable Debt Payment Rate*

(Coop@ _____% = $_____ per mo. Condo@_____% = $_____ per mo.)

Monthly Debt Cost	$_____	$_____	$_____

Maintenance/Common Charge

	$_____	$_____	$_____

Real Estate Tax *(condo only)*

	$_____	$_____	$_____
Cash per Month	$_____	$_____	$_____

Condominiums have a lower interest rate by .5% than cooperatives unless the buyer utilizes deep leverage (90% financing) in which case the rate is the same for both.

The Applied Science of Buying an Apartment

Applying the strategy described in the preceding chapter will provide a clearer sense of the procedure in action.

Gina and Alan Green are considering buying an apartment. They are married and want to start a family. They both work, giving them a combined income of $200,000, and they have accumulated $250,000 in cash. They undertake the following procedure.

FILLING IN THE WORKSHEETS

Step 1: Developing Parameters for each Primary Motivator
The Greens fill in the worksheets. They begin by defining the parameters for each of the Primary Motivators, grading each element according to its relative importance in their overall purchasing decision. Elements such as Cityscape Views would be wonderful to have, but the Greens must decide how integral it is to their decision to have such views. If it's critical, then they grade it a "10." If it's inconsequential, then they might grade it a "3." If there are any elements they definitely don't want, they would give these a grade of "1."

Step 2: Defining the Range

After defining the Parameters, the Greens must determine: "What would be the worst qualities for this criteria?" This is a "1." "What would be the ideal for this criteria?" This is a "10." And, "what would be the middle ground for this criteria?" This is a "5." They put these descriptions into words to clearly define their feelings.

Step 3: Defining Flexibility

The Greens now consider the absolute minimal level for each Primary Motivator that they could accept. They should assume that *all other* features of the apartment are ideal. For example, in the case of Light, the Greens determine that if every other quality of the apartment was optimal, they would be willing to buy an apartment with indirect light facing a street, but they are not willing to buy a dark apartment facing a courtyard.

Step 4: Identifying Secondary Factors

The Greens decide that there are no material Secondary Factors in their decision-making process.

PRIMARY MOTIVATORS WORKSHEET
LOCATION

Location refers to the area in which the building is situated and includes aesthetics, services, transportation, and reputation measures, among others.

Define the Parameters: Grade the relative importance to your overall purchasing decision of each item below, "1" being undesirable, "10" being optimal. Intervening grades (2, 3, 4, 5, 6, 7, 8, 9) express an interim level of importance.

Tree-lined streets	8	Restaurants and culture	5
Proximity to subways	7	Noise level	6
Commercial/residential mix	7	Single/couple/family mix	8
Perceived reputation of area	5	Shopping	5
Historic ambiance of block	7	Proximity to parks	7

Define the Range: Utilizing these parameters, create a general statement expressing your overall position on location, "1" being undesirable, "10" being optimal.

A grade "1" location is: _No trees, no families, far from subways, no proximity to parks, no ambiance._

A grade "10" location is: _Tree-lined street, close to subways and shopping, residential character, historic ambiance, close to parks._

A grade "5" location is: _Tree-lined street, some commercial elements, slightly noisy, no reputation._

Define your Flexibility: How important is Location in the context of all your other criteria?

Assuming all other elements were optimal, I would not buy an apartment if the Location grade was below ___4___

PRIMARY MOTIVATORS WORKSHEET
BUILDING

Building refers to a specific property, and includes its aesthetic qualities, condition, services, building-wide amenities and perceived reputation.

Define the Parameters: Grade the relative importance to your overall purchasing decision of each item below, "1" being undesirable, "10" being optimal. Intervening grades (2, 3, 4, 5, 6, 7, 8, 9) express an interim level of importance.

Perceived building reputation	3	Architectural detail	5
Modern	8	Prewar	7
Garage in building	5	Elevator	10
Building condition	8	Common outdoor space	3
Hi-rise	5	Pool/health club	5
Concierge	3	Doormen	10

Define the Range: Utilizing these parameters, create a general statement expressing your overall position on Building, "1" being undesirable, "10" being optimal.

A grade "1" building is: _Poor condition, no doorman, no elevator._

A grade "10" building is: _Excellent condition, doorman, elevator, health club, modern design._

A grade "5" building is: _Good condition, doorman, elevator, average amenities._

Define your Flexibility: How important is the Building in the context of all your other criteria?

Assuming all other elements were optimal, I would not buy an apartment if the Building grade was below ___4___

AIR AND LAYOUT

Air and Layout relate to the sense of openness of the apartment and the organization of the rooms.

Define the Parameters: Grade the relative importance to your overall purchasing decision of each item below, "1" being undesirable, "10" being optimal. Intervening grades (2, 3, 4, 5, 6, 7, 8, 9) express an interim level of importance.

High ceilings	5	Eat-in kitchen	8
Separate dining room	1	Entry foyer	3
Maid's room	0		

Define the Range: Not applicable.

Define your Flexibility: How important are Air and Layout in the context of your other criteria?

Assuming all other elements were optimal, I would not buy an apartment if the following elements of Air and Layout were missing: _Would be willing to forgo eat-in kitchen if necessary; average ceiling heights are acceptable,_

PRIMARY MOTIVATORS WORKSHEET
LIGHT

Light consists of two elements: **floor height** and the **predominant view** (typically determined by the living room window).

Determine the lowest floor on which you would live: __2__

Define the Parameters: Grade the relative importance to your overall purchasing decision of each item below, "1" being undesirable, "10" being optimal. Intervening grades (2, 3, 4, 5, 6, 7, 8, 9) express an interim level of importance.

Cityscape view	__7__	Park view	__7__
River view	__7__	Local street view	__5__
Commercial street view	__5__	Building across street view	__5__
Courtyard view	__1__	Direct sun	__7__

Define the Range: Utilizing these parameters, create a general statement expressing your overall position on Light, "1" being undesirable, "10" being optimal.

A grade "1" view is: _A view of a courtyard that is dark, on a low floor._

A grade "10" view is: _A panoramic cityscape view, high floor._

A grade "5" view is: _A view of a local street, fifth floor._

Define your Flexibility: How important is the View in the context of all your other criteria?

Assuming all other elements were optimal, I would not buy an apartment if the View grade was below __4__

PRIMARY MOTIVATORS WORKSHEET
SPACE

Space is not the total area in the apartment. Rather, it is the area contained in the "Value Rooms:" the Living Room, Dining Area and Master Bedroom.

Desired Living Room size	30	× 12	= 360	sq. ft.
Desired Dining Area size (optional)	_____	× _____	= _____	sq. ft.
Desired Master Bedroom size	18	× 12	= 216	sq. ft.
Space of the Value Rooms		TOTAL	= 576	sq. ft.

Define your Flexibility: How important is Space in the context of all your other criteria?

Assuming all other elements were optimal, I would not buy an apartment if the Space parameters were less than:

Living Room size	20	× 12	= 240	sq. ft.
Dining Area size (optional)	_____	× _____	= _____	sq. ft.
Master Bedroom size	16	× 12	= 182	sq. ft.

PRIMARY MOTIVATORS WORKSHEET
SECONDARY FACTORS

Secondary factors are additional features which are not integral to the decision-making process unless the minimal requirements of Location, Building, Air and Layout, Light and Space have first been satisfied. These items do not need to be graded; simply check off or add other desired items.

Wood-burning fireplace ( )   Terraces and outdoor space ( )

___n/a_____   ___n/a_____

_____   _____

Step 5: Determining Cash Down Payment

The Greens estimate that they will be buying an apartment for approximately $650,000. They know they must retain a cash reserve after the purchase, so they decide to take 10% of their projected purchase price, $65,000, as the amount to set aside from their total available cash of $250,000, leaving $185,000 available as equity to buy an apartment. They enter this on the bottom section of the Buyer Formula Work Sheet under Cash Down Payment.

One of the rules a bank uses to determine what it will lend on a mortgage for a home is the Debt/Equity Rule. This provides that 25% of the purchase price must come from an equity down payment. Accordingly, the implied price the Greens can afford under this rule is $740,000 (four times their equity cash payment).

Step 6: Determining Cost Per Month

The Greens' Gross Income is $200,000. When they multiply this amount by 30% they arrive at a sum most coop boards consider reasonable for the annual carrying cost of a home: $60,000. Dividing this by 12, they arrive at a monthly figure of $5,000. They know they could borrow more for a condominium, and will consider that in their final evaluation after they have completed their comparative analysis.

After studying the ads for coop apartments for sale in their price range, they determine that a rough estimate of the maintenance charge they will have to pay is $1,200 per month. By subtracting this sum from the $5,000 available monthly for their home carrying cost, they find they have $3,800 per month available for supporting a loan on the property.

The Greens think they will be able to obtain a 9% fixed rate mortgage for a term of 30 years. They go to the schedule on page 116 and determine that the monthly cost of carrying this rate of interest is $8.05 per thousand. They compute the amount of mortgage a bank would lend them under the Bank Carrying Cost Rule by dividing the sum available to carry monthly debt, $3,800, by the debt service percentage on a dollar of that debt per month, .00805. This computation leads to a mortgage amount of $472,050. That, plus the $185,000 they intend to use as a down payment, would imply a home price of $657,050.

By comparing the mortgage money that a bank would lend them under the Debt/Equity Rule (down payment based) and the Bank Carrying Cost Rule (income based), the Greens determine that their income is the limiting factor in their purchase. The Greens know that there is flexibility in the bank rules, so they conclude that their price range will be approximately $600,000 to $700,000.

Step 7: Creating your Buying Formula

In reviewing their analysis of the five Primary Motivators, the Greens have developed their "recipe" for the apartment they want. They would like to have a location that is an 8 in a building that is a 7. They would prefer to have an eat-in kitchen, to live above the 8th floor, and have a view that is a 6. They also want a Living Room of 24 × 12 and a Master Bedroom of 18 × 12.

This buyer formula is intended to define benchmarks against which the Greens can measure prospective apartments. They can compare the merits of each apartment against this standard in order to evaluate which one best suits their overall needs.

BUYER FORMULA WORKSHEET
PRIMARY MOTIVATORS

Desired Location grade ___8___ Desired Building grade ___7___
Desired Air and Layout features _Eat-in kitchen_____
Desired Floor ___8th___ Desired View grade ___6___
Space:
    Desired Living Room size ___26__ × __12___
    Desired Dining Room size (optional) _____ × _____
    Desired Master Bedroom size ___18__ × __12___

Secondary Factors_ _None_____

FINANCIAL MOTIVATORS

Cash Down Payment	$ 185,000
Debt Equity Rule Multiplier	×4
The Implied Price using Bank Debt/Equity Bank Rule	$ 740,000
Cost Per Month (30% of Gross Income divided by 12)	$ 5,000
Less: Estimated Maintenance Charge	$ 1,200
Available for Monthly Debt Payment	$ 3,800
Divide by: Debt Interest Factor (see chart on page 116)	.00805 %
Implied Mortgage under Bank Carrying Cost Rule	$ 472,050
Add: Invested Cash Down Payment	$ 185,000
Implied Price using the Bank's 30% Carrying Cost Rule	$ 657,050

Price Range Guide $____600,000____ to $____700,000____

DECIDING BETWEEN ALTERNATIVES

After seeing a number of apartments, the Greens have narrowed their search to three alternatives.

Apartment A:
Property A is located in the mid-50s on the West Side of Manhattan. It is in a prewar building in good condition. The location is busy, and there are many poorly maintained tenement buildings nearby, but the apartment is two blocks from Central Park South and has panoramic views facing south. The living room is 22 × 12 and the master bedroom is 18 × 12. There is an eat-in kitchen. The asking price is $620,000, and the maintenance charge is $1,220 per month.

Apartment B:
Property B is located on the Upper West Side of Manhattan in the 80s in a prewar, doorman building in good condition. It is on West End Avenue, which is one block east of Riverside Park and one block west of Broadway. The location is busy, but has an appealing residential character. The apartment is bright, but the view is of the apartment building across the street. There is a large living room, 28 × 12, and the master bedroom is 18 × 12. There is an eat-in kitchen. The price of the apartment is $650,000 and the maintenance is $960 per month.

Apartment C:
Property C is located on East End Avenue on the East Side of Manhattan. It is in a new condominium building and has views of the East River. The location is quiet, and across the street from Carl Schurz Park. The services to the neighborhood are somewhat distant: a walk of five blocks to the subway and four blocks to the supermarket. The apartment is on the 6th floor. It has a living room of 22 × 12 and a master bedroom of 17 × 11. The asking price is $700,000 and the common charges are $650 per month with real estate taxes of $450 per month, for a total monthly cost of $1,100.

The Greens are now able to put together their comparative analysis.

BUYER FORMULA WORKSHEET

COMPARATIVE WORKSHEET FOR VIABLE APARTMENTS

Address	APARTMENT A	APARTMENT B	APARTMENT C
Location Grade	5	8	8
Building Grade	8	7	10
Air Qualities	EIK/2 bath	EIK/2 bath	No EIK/2 bath
Light			
View Grade	8	6	9
Floor	12th	8th	6th
Space			
Living Room	22 × 12	28 × 12	22 × 12
Dining Room	___ × ___	___ × ___	___ × ___
Master Bedroom	18 × 12	18 × 12	17 × 11
Secondary Factors	_____	_____	_____
Asking Price	$ 620,000	$ 650,000	$ 700,000
Cash Down	$ 155,000	$ 162,500	$ 175,000
Mortgage Amount	$ 465,000	$ 487,500	$ 525,000

Applicable Debt Payment Rate*

(Coop@ __9__ % = $.00805 per mo. Condo@ 8.5 % = $ .00769 per mo.)

Monthly Debt Cost	$ 3,743	$ 3,924	$ 4,037

Maintenance/Common Charge

	$ 1,220	$ 960	$ 650

Real Estate Tax (condo only)

	$_____	$_____	$ 450
Cash per Month	$ 4,963	$ 4,884	$ 5,137

Condominiums have a lower interest rate by .5% than cooperatives, unless the buyer utilizes deep leverage (90% financing), in which case the rate is the same for both.

THE GREEN'S DECISION

Comparing the Apartments:

In evaluating these three alternatives, the Greens can come to some conclusions in light of their buyer formula and their financial limitations. It is important to remember that their decision might be different from yours. Every buyer is unique.

The Greens decide that Apartment A is in a substantially inferior location to the other two and to their buying formula. They decide to eliminate it. Apartment C is not as large as specified in the buying formula, nor as large as Apartment B. Space is an important factor to the Greens, and is their Crucial Determinant (the first and foremost item on their recipe list). The high value for Apartment C's building grade is not enough to warrant the Greens selecting it, particularly since Apartment C does not have an eat-in kitchen. They therefore decide that Apartment B is their best choice.

Adjusting for Actual Down Payment Cash:

The Green's buyer formula allows for a carrying cost of $5,000 per month and a cash down payment of $185,000. For Apartment B, the Comparative Worksheet For Viable Apartments assumes a carrying cost of $4,884 per month and a cash down payment of $162,500. By investing the entire $185,000 they could reduce both the mortgage amount and their carrying costs, for a savings of $181.12 per month. This was calculated as follows:

Buyer Formula Invested Cash	$ 185,000
Apartment B Required Cash	− 162,500
Additional Available Funds	$ 22,500
Mortgage Factor	× .00805
Monthly Savings	$ 181.12

Decision:

To make an offer for Apartment B and to use the entire $185,000 cash for the down payment in order to reduce the monthly carrying cost to approximately $4,703.

Understanding the Contract

DISCLAIMER

This is a summary of the material provisions of the Standard Form Cooperative Contract, normally referred to as Blumberg Form M123. Blumberg contracts are the predominant forms used in New York City for the transfer of cooperative and condominium apartments. The distinguishing features between this contract form and that used for condominiums, Blumberg Form 146, are discussed at the end of this chapter. This outline is not intended to be a legal authority. Rather, it is an encapsulation of the material issues presented in the contract. **Anyone buying or selling property should see a lawyer for professional guidance and expertise.**

BASIC INFORMATION

On the first page of the contract, the buyer and seller make a number of representations. These include identifying the buying and selling parties and their attorneys, identifying the apartment being sold and the party who will hold the contract deposit (referred to as the escrow agent, normally the seller's attorney), identifying the broker, stating the current maintenance fee, and disclosing any open assessments levied on the apartment. If there is a transfer charge levied by the cooperative corporation (referred to as a flip tax), the party who is responsible for making that payment will be noted. The contract stipulates whether or not the purchase is contingent on the buyer obtaining financing and, if so, the amount of that loan. Additionally, the buyer identifies the proposed occupants and if there will be any pets.

A number of these points deserve further consideration. The first relates to the **Escrow.** These contract deposit funds are normally held in a regular checking account and do not bear interest. This is because the State of New York does not permit an escrow agent to commingle funds from different clients into a common interest-bearing account. If the client specifies that the escrow account should be interest-bearing, the escrow agent must open a separate account specifically for that purpose. Normally, the cost of the time and effort involved exceeds the benefits unless the contract deposit is unusually large or the length of time between the contract and the closing unusually long. In those rare instances when an interest-bearing account is used, the interest on the escrow funds usually accrue to the benefit of the buyer, although this can be a point of negotiation.

Another issue is the **Flip Tax.** The name is deceptive since it isn't a tax and nothing is necessarily being "flipped." Basically, a flip tax is a charge levied by the cooperative corporation on the transfer of ownership of an apartment, and serves as a means of generating income for the building. The seller customarily makes the flip tax payment, but the contract is silent on this point in order to permit flexibility in negotiations between the parties. The flip tax is normally a percentage of the sales price, and usually ranges from one to three percent.

Pets are another touchy issue in many coops. If an owner is allowed to keep a pet in the apartment, it should say so clearly in the contract particularly since many buildings do not permit pets. Don't assume that because you have seen a resident with a dog in the lobby that the building permits pets. It may be "grandfathered" under an old rule and new owners may not be entitled to the same privileges. The term "pet" does not refer only to dogs, but also to cats, birds, or any other type of animal.

The **Occupants** of the apartment should be spelled out in the contract, especially if they are not the owners. There is bound to be controversy if the prospective owners are interviewed and accepted into the building as residents, but then someone else (a relative, for instance) occupies the apartment instead. This is an issue that should be resolved at the earliest possible moment with the board of directors and/or the building's managing agent.

In clause two of the standard contract, the **Price** of the apartment is stated and the **Terms** of payment defined. The terms are normally a 10% deposit due on signing the contract with the balance due in certified funds on the closing date — usually 60 to 90 days after the contract is signed. At times, when banks are overwhelmed with mortgage applications, the date can extend to as long as 120 days. Normally, a buyer can get a 30-day extension of the closing date without fear of adverse consequences under protections afforded through New York State law. Extensions beyond that are solely at the discretion of the seller. If the contract specifically states that "time is of the essence," no extensions will be permitted to the buyer, and he or she must close by the stated date.

In the period between the signing of the contract and the closing, the buyer must obtain board approval, arrange for financing, and make arrangements to finalize any other open issues related to purchasing the apartment.

There are things in the apartment, referred to as **Personal Property,** that are customarily transferred as part of the purchase. The legal definition of real estate is "land and anything permanently affixed thereto." Personal property is everything not "permanently affixed thereto." Accordingly, the contract will state that the kitchen appliances, cabinetry, air conditioners, lights, and wall-to-wall carpeting are included. If there is a washing machine and dryer, the contract states that these should also stay. If the windows have screens and window treatments, these are included as well. Even hardware such as doorknobs, door stops, handles and bells are specified as part of the deal.

The contract stops there. Nothing else will be transferred to the buyer unless specifically provided for in the contract. This includes, for example, any special built-ins, furnishings, or pictures. It is not uncommon for disagreements to arise regarding what is and what is not included in a deal. In many instances the seller will wish to remove items that the contract form stipulates as included. A wise buyer should assume that nothing is included unless the contract expressly says it is. All understandings between the buyer and the seller should be spelled out in the contract in clearly defined terms.

REPRESENTATIONS AND PROMISES

The contract calls for the sellers to make certain representations about the nature of their ownership. The **Sellers** must represent that they are the **sole owners** and that they are in good standing with the cooperative corporation. Sellers must also affirm that they have the **right to sell** the apartment and will do so free of any liens or encumbrances. Furthermore, the sellers must represent that there will be **no money owed** on the apartment at the time of transfer. Finally, the sellers must assert that they have **done nothing wrong** during their tenancy which would adversely affect the subsequent owners, and that they **have not received any notices** about assessments or increases in the maintenance.

Buyers, in turn, must assure sellers that they have **looked at all the documents** necessary for making their purchasing decision or that they **waive examination** of those documents as a condition for going through with the transaction.

REQUIRED APPROVAL

In cooperative corporations, the sale of any apartment is subject to approval by the board of directors. The contract states that the buyer must submit an application and any other required documents to the board within ten days of signing the agreement and, within three days of receiving a loan commitment, the buyer shall submit proof of the commitment.

These **deadlines** are often difficult or impossible to meet. Preparing the application and gathering financial reports, reference letters, and supporting documents takes a substantial amount of time. In addition, if the deal is subject to financing, boards will rarely accept an application for review until it includes a commitment letter from a bank. It is therefore suggested that if the application is not subject to financing, the term for submission of the application should be 30 days from the signing of the contract. If the contract includes financing, the term for submission should be ten days after receipt of the commitment letter (receipt of the commitment letter has specific date limitations).

In addition to submitting the application and supporting documents, the buyer must attend a board **interview**. Many prospective buyers fear the interview process, but in the vast majority of cases boards are respectful, friendly, and even welcoming. Indeed, many buyers become more committed to the purchase after having met the board and having seen who their neighbors will be. However, there are at least a few buyers with war stories to tell, so it's a good idea to consider the following before attending a board interview:

- *Don't be angry or indignant.*
- *Don't use this as a forum to espouse any social or political philosophy.*
- *Dress in business attire and look professional.*
- *If you are asked a question which you think is inappropriate, try to remain diplomatic in your response. If you have strong feelings about the question, it might be appropriate to address the issue with a board member on an informal basis — after you have closed and moved into the building.*
- *Review your financial documents before the meeting so that you can answer any questions that may be posed about them intelligently.*
- *Be yourself. Don't try to be overly impressive or overly humble.*

RISK OF LOSS

The contract states that the apartment is to be sold "as is," that it will be delivered "broom clean," and that the appliances will be in "working order."

In the event that damage occurs in the apartment prior to the closing, it is the responsibility of the seller to fix it. Sometimes the damage is substantial. In this case, the seller can elect to restore the apartment within sixty days after notifying the buyer, or the buyer can accept the apartment in its current condition and receive any insurance proceeds relating to the loss. If there has been a significant loss and the seller refuses to repair it, the buyer can elect to get out of the agreement. In the event that the buyer, or anyone responsible to the buyer, performed the act that caused the damage, the risk of loss is borne by the buyer.

The risk of loss provision covers some serious issues. What happens if, when moving out, the seller's movers damage a wall, the floor, or some other part of the apartment? Customary practice is that a sum of money, representing a reasonable estimate of the cost of the repair, remains in escrow. The buyer then makes the repair and submits the bill to the seller's attorney for reimbursement. If the amount of the bill is less than the amount held in escrow, the balance goes to the seller. If the amount of the bill is greater than the amount in escrow, the buyer must absorb the shortfall.

THE CLOSING

The location of the closing will be designated by the coop corporation.

The Seller shall deliver the following at closing:
* *the shares of stock and proprietary lease*
* *a statement permitting the transfer of the shares, signed by the appropriate representative of the cooperative corporation*
* *all necessary tax documents associated with the transfer*
* *other documents, as specifically noted and required under the contract*
* *the keys to the apartment*

The Buyer shall do the following at the closing:
* *deliver a certified check for the remainder of the funds due*
* *execute and deliver new stock and proprietary lease (or assignments of the existing stock and lease)*
* *provide tax documents and any other documents that are required under the contract*

In addition, at the closing an apportionment of maintenance is paid by the seller for the period running through the prior day. If an assessment is due, the contract states that if the due date is prior to closing, it will be paid by the seller, and if it is subsequent to closing, it will be paid by the buyer.

Then, usually by separate agreement, the real estate broker will be paid his or her commission.

DEFAULTS, REMEDIES AND OTHER LIMITATIONS

If either party breaches the agreement, the remedies are simple and clear:
- *If the buyer defaults, the seller can keep the buyer's 10% down payment.*
- *If the seller defaults, the buyer can either bring an action at law to compel performance under the contract or the buyer can sue for monetary damages.*
- *The parties to the sale and to the purchase indemnify each other against breaches to the contract made by one or the other. This means that any claim made by a third party adversely affected by the breach is the responsibility of the violating party.*
- *The contract stands as the total agreement. No oral statements made by either party can be enforced unless they have been placed in writing in the agreement.*
- *The agreement cannot be assigned to another party.*
- *Nothing represented in the agreement survives the closing unless expressly stated in the contract.*
- *The buyer can inspect the apartment within 48 hours of the closing.*
- *The parties agree to act in good faith.*

FINANCING CONTINGENCY

If financing is a condition of the agreement, the buyer must diligently apply for a loan within seven days after the contract is executed. The contract can be cancelled, and the buyer's down payment returned, if any of the following three conditions occur:
- *A loan commitment letter is not obtained by the date specified in the contract.*
- *The bank is unable to obtain a letter from the cooperative corporation recognizing its secured interest under terms the bank finds satisfactory.*
- *The closing is extended by the seller or the cooperative corporation by more than 30 days, the commitment letter expires during this period, and the buyer cannot get an extension without making an additional payment. However, this provision can be overcome if the seller agrees to make that payment on the buyer's behalf.*

If the buyer seeks to cancel the contract, he or she must give legal notice within seven days of the date that the right of cancellation initiates. Legal notice must be in writing, and either delivered by hand, overnight mail, or sent by certified or registered mail to the seller and the seller's attorney.

It is extremely important that the conditions under the financing contingency be carefully monitored. In the event that the commitment date on the contract passes and the buyer has not provided legal notice to the seller and the seller's attorney, the contract is no longer subject to financing, and the buyer must perform under the terms of the contract or lose his or her deposit. The dates are critical, as well as the form of giving notice.

DISTINGUISHING FEATURES BETWEEN THE COOPERATIVE CONTRACT AND THE CONDOMINIUM CONTRACT

Attorneys involved in a condominium sale normally use Blumberg Form M146. This contract is substantially similar in content to the contract described above except for the following items:

Condominium Unit Deed: A condominium buyer receives a deed rather than stock and a lease. Additionally, the seller must identify the real estate taxes on the unit, since these taxes are paid separately by the condominium unit owner. Furthermore, the monthly charge is referred to as a common charge rather than a maintenance charge.

Approval: Normally, no condominium board approval is required for purchasing a condominium. However, a Right of First Refusal procedure is common. This Right of First Refusal permits the condominium board to review the contract and to request information about the purchaser. There are many occasions where this review can be as extensive an inquiry as that required by a cooperative board. If the condominium board objects to the purchaser, it may refuse to permit the sale. However, the condominium is then compelled to buy the unit under the same terms and conditions as expressed in the rejected contract.

Title Insurance: Since a condominium is real estate, it is important that the title be free of claims by third parties. A review of the title must be performed, and insurance obtained to protect against any claims of which the buyer is unaware. The title search is done by a title abstract company which will also issue, for a fee, title insurance that guarantees the new owner protection from any future claims made by third parties against the title.

The Prospectus

PART 1:
THE STANDARD PROCEDURE FOR CONVERTING A BUILDING TO COOPERATIVE OR CONDOMINIUM OWNERSHIP

THE OFFERING PLAN

The **Offering Plan**, also referred to as the **Prospectus** or **Black Book**, is prepared by the owner of the building being converted to cooperative/condominium ownership. It is intended to assist buyers in making an informed decision about the prospective purchase of an apartment. Before it can be distributed to the public, the Offering Plan must be reviewed by the New York State Attorney General's Office to insure the information it contains is complete and accurate in accordance with New York State legal requirements.

Once the Attorney General's office determines that the Offering Plan is in compliance, it is "Accepted for Filing" and can be distributed to prospective buyers. However, the mere fact that an Offering Plan meets minimum legal standards of disclosure should not be construed as an endorsement of its terms, conditions, or offering prices by any government authority. Therefore, "*caveat emptor*" or "let the buyer beware" are still the watchwords for any potential purchaser.

During the course of the conversion procedure, it is not unusual for the **Sponsor** — the owner, who initiates the conversion — to make alterations in the price and/or terms of the offer. In such a case, the sponsor must file an Amendment to the Plan which must also be approved by the State Attorney General's Office. These **Amendments** are an integral part of the Offering Plan which should be reviewed by interested buyers. Amendments may be filed even after the date of conversion to cooperative or condominium ownership if the sponsor has a continuing economic interest in the property and proposes a revised offer for selling apartments to tenant-occupants. Additionally, the State Attorney General requires ongoing yearly disclosure by any party having a material interest that exceeds 10% of the shares of the corporation, whether it be the sponsor or a third party investor. This yearly disclosure must include financial information about the party.

FORMS OF OWNERSHIP

Generally, buildings change to unit ownership through conversion of existing rental property, new construction, or rehabilitation. In its most simple terms, a **Cooperative Conversion** is the sale of a building to a newly formed corporation. The original owner, the landlord, becomes the sponsor, and he or she initiates the process by creating an Offering Plan promoting the sale of **Stock** in the new corporation. The purchaser gains residency rights by means of a proprietary lease relating to each specific apartment that is appurtenant to the stock ownership.

In a **Condominium**, the Offering Plan proposes the partition of the building's ownership into unit interests. Each purchaser acquires an apartment and receives a **Unit Deed**. In addition, a Master Deed and the Bylaws describe the rights and obligations of both the Condominium Association and the unit owners to the building's common areas and services. Condominiums in New York are governed by Article 9B of the New York Real Property Law, commonly known as the New York Condominium Act.

THE MARTIN ACT

The law in New York State regulating the process of conversion to cooperative and condominium ownership is referred to as The Martin Act, and can be found in Sections 352eee and 352eeee of New York State's General Business Law. Under the provisions of this act, a building may be converted to cooperative ownership if 15% of the shares of stock in the new corporation are subscribed to and transferred. In the case of a condominium, a similar percentage of unit deed interests must be transferred.

The law also provides for an alternate conversion form, referred to as an **Eviction Plan**, wherein 51% of the tenants in occupancy must subscribe, and the nonsubscribing tenants must leave their apartments at the end of their lease terms. Years ago, the threshold percentage for an Eviction Plan was 35%, and Eviction Plans were common. Under current rules, eviction plans are rarely employed.

The law mandates that allocation of shares of stock in a cooperative corporation, or unit interests in a condominium be assigned to specific apartments, and this **allocation of shares** (i.e., the percentage of the total number of shares for the building assigned to each specific apartment) be "rational and reasonable." Therefore, the 15% rule effectively mandates transfer of property ownership of approximately this same percentage before an Offering Plan can be declared effective. By law, each cooperative apartment must receive along with the shares a **Proprietary Lease** that gives the shareholder the right to occupy a specific apartment. In a condominium conversion, the deed covering the entire property is partitioned into unit interests, and each apartment is allocated a percentage of the whole, also on a rational and reasonable basis.

The law requires the sponsor to offer tenants in occupancy the first **right to purchase** the shares allocated to their apartments. As a result, landlords frequently offer tenants a discounted purchase price to encourage them to buy the apartments they have been renting. However, the tenant has no obligation to purchase. Under a **15% Non-Eviction Plan**, if the apartment is covered by New York State rent regulations, the tenant may continue to live in it for as long as he or she desires. This remains true even if the apartment is sold to a third party.

Occasionally, a group of people acquire a building together, each investor is allocated an apartment, and no units are offered to outside purchasers. On these rare occasions, the New York State Attorney General's Office will issue a **No-Action Letter**, effectively permitting the conversion to cooperative ownership without the filing of an offering plan. Accordingly, any later purchaser will not be able to review a plan, since none was initially developed.

DECLARING THE PLAN EFFECTIVE

If the 15% threshold is met, the landlord will issue a **Declaration of Effectiveness.** This is the sponsor's pronouncement that statutory requirements have been met and that the conversion is now in effect, subject to final closing on all subscriptions for the purchase of stock (or unit deeds in the case of a condominium) and the transfer of funds. When all subscription agreements are closed, the cooperative corporation will transfer the funds to the landlord in exchange for the deed to the property. When apartments remain unpurchased, the landlord takes the **Unsold Shares** as additional payment to conclude the transfer of ownership of the property. In a condominium, the procedure is essentially the same, except the landlord is given condominium unit interests instead of shares and leases for the unsold apartments.

Therefore, even if a landlord/sponsor continues to have an economic interest in the property, all the apartments have been transferred to the coop corporation (or condo association) for the purpose of effectuating the conversion. All of the apartments have equal rights and obligations, subject to their respective share allocation or their unit deed percentage interest.

A SUMMARY OF THE CONVERSION PROCESS

In a nutshell, the conversion process goes like this:

1. A Preliminary Offering Plan, *referred to as a* **"Red Herring,"** *is issued to all tenants; it is an informational book advising tenants of the prospective offer.*

2. *The State Attorney General's Office reviews the proposed* **Prospectus** *(also called the Offering Plan or Black Book) and accepts the plan for filing. Thereafter, the* **Offering Plan** *is officially issued.*

3. Negotiations *on price and terms begin between the landlord and the Tenants.* **Amendments** *are filed with the State Attorney General's office to advise of any changes in the initial offering terms.*

4. Subscriptions *(agreements to purchase) are signed by tenants in occupancy and outside parties for shares of stock (coops), or condominium unit interests (condo). A minimum of 15% must sign for the landlord to declare the plan effective.*

5. *All tenants and outside parties* **fully pay up their subscriptions** *and, in the case of a coop, receive stock in the cooperative corporation and a lease to a specific apartment, or, in the case of a condo, a unit deed.*

6. *The* **deed to the entire property is transferred** *and the landlord receives the cash from the sale of all subscribed shares as well as the unsold shares on apartments not purchased in a coop, or unit deeds on unpurchased apartments in a condo.*

PART 2:
MATERIAL COMPONENTS OF THE PROSPECTUS

1.

SCHEDULE A
SHARE ALLOCATIONS OR UNIT INTERESTS

Each apartment is allocated shares of stock. The shares of the apartments, in total, comprise the full number of outstanding shares in the cooperative corporation (or unit percentage interest, in the case of a condominium). The actual number of shares allocated to any specific apartment is meaningless. Rather, it is the **apartment's fractional interest** to the total shares outstanding that is relevant. Section 216 of the U.S. Internal Revenue Code and the New York State Martin Act require that the apartment's allocation of shares bear a **reasonable relationship** to the total. This term "reasonable relationship" is open to interpretation, but generally it means that the allocation of a coop's shares is based on the relative fair market value of the apartments. In condominiums, a reasonable relationship is typically based on square footage and other factors meaningful to value. Under the Martin Act, the share allocations for a cooperative or unit percentage interests for a condominium must be certified as rational and reasonable by an independent expert. This opinion letter, referred to as a **Letter of Reasonable Relationship**, is normally prepared by a real estate broker familiar with values in the area. It also can be found in the Offering Plan.

The share or unit interest allocation is given in Schedule A of the Offering Plan. Schedule A normally includes the apartment number, the number of rooms, the allocated number of shares (or unit percentage interest in a condominium), the portion of the underlying mortgage of the building allocated to the unit, the initial maintenance charge (or common charge in a condominium), the allocated portion of the real estate taxes on the building, and the allocated portion of the building's tax deductible interest.

2.

SCHEDULE B
FIRST-YEAR OPERATING BUDGET

An Offering Plan must present an **Operating Budget** for the first year of operation. This budget, outlined in Schedule B of the Offering Plan, estimates an amount for each expense item, along with accompanying notes explaining how these amounts were determined. In newly constructed buildings, generous expense estimates are the norm since they are based on input from outside engineers and consultants who tend to evaluate costs conservatively. The sponsor may also favor conservatism since, under current state regulations, the sponsor may be held responsible if the building has an economic shortfall.

When a building is converting from rental to ownership, the state requires that the Offering Plan include audited financial statements for prior years. Since rental buildings are often run more frugally than coops and condos, it is common that the projected maintenance charges expressed in Schedule B are less than the actual amount owners will eventually pay in future years. This is somewhat ameliorated by a provision found in many offering plans restricting the right of the cooperative corporation to increase services and amenities during the initial stages of the conversion without consent of the sponsor.

Under New York State law, an expert must certify the proposed operating budget as adequate to cover all costs for the first year of operation. A property management company familiar with costs of operation in the local area will normally prepare this **Letter of Adequacy** which is found in the Offering Plan.

3.
TAX OPINION LETTER

Under Section 216 of the Internal Revenue Code, tenant-shareholders of cooperative corporations are entitled to **deduct** on their personal tax returns their allocable portion of real estate taxes and interest paid by the cooperative corporation. However, there are certain qualifying criteria which the coop must meet in order to be entitled to pass-through these deductions. These criteria are as follows:

1. *The corporation must have only one class of stock outstanding.*

2. *Each stockholder must be entitled, solely by reason of ownership of stock in the corporation, to occupy, for dwelling purposes, an apartment in the building owned by the cooperative corporation.*

3. *No stockholder of the corporation may be entitled to a distribution not out of earnings and profits, except in complete or partial liquidation of the cooperative corporation.*

4. *80% or more of the Gross Income of the corporation each year must be derived from the tenant-stockholders.*

In addition to federal tax advantages, New York City also offers certain tax programs to qualifying buildings. The nature and qualifications for these programs vary from time to time, but are primarily as follows:

421 A — *This program is for newly constructed buildings and permits a phase-*

in of real estate taxes over a ten-year period. Currently, the program is available only on a limited basis, but many previously qualifying properties are still in their phase-in period.

J-51 — This program is for buildings undergoing substantial rehabilitation. The program provides for an abatement of real estate taxes for a certain term, and then an exclusion from additional taxes for an additional term based on the change in property use and the level of improvement. The level of adjustment is determined by a formula set by the city which changes from time to time. The program is still available, but only in certain areas of the city. However, the phase-out period still continues for many properties.

In the Prospectus, a **Tax Opinion Letter**, prepared by a tax expert/attorney, must define the rights of each coop tenant-shareholder to the benefits prescribed by Section 216 of the Internal Revenue Code, as well as any benefits associated with state tax programs. For condominiums, the tax opinion letter describes the tax features specific to condominium ownership.

4.

ENGINEER'S REPORT

An engineer must evaluate the condition of the building and issue a **Certified Engineer's Report** in which all physical aspects of the building are commented on, and any building code violations specifically identified. It is not necessary for the sponsor to correct any of the reported deficiencies unless they are extremely onerous. Rather, the report must provide full disclosure. In addition, the engineer must estimate the cost of correcting any identified problems.

Frequently, in a building converting from rental to ownership, the tenants will hire their own engineer, whose findings are often significantly different from that of the sponsor's engineer. Each report differs as to the nature of defects and the appropriate remedies, usually reflecting the bias of the party it represents. When two reports are prepared, the Attorney General may require that both be presented in the Offering Plan.

Although the Engineer's Report is extremely important in the conversion process, its usefulness is of limited duration, since the evaluation reflects the condition of the property only at the time of inspection. Repairs and/or additional defects could have occurred since the date of the report. Generally, a report more than five years old is considered obsolete. If the report is less than five years old, it should be evaluated in conjunction with other documents, such as the minutes of the board of directors and the financial statements of the cooperative corporation or condominium, which would outline changes since the Engineer's Report was generated.

5.
IDENTIFICATION OF THE PARTIES

The Attorney General requires that the party initiating the Offering Plan, the sponsor, must be clearly identified. This identification must include the **individuals** — owners, partners, and material investors — who are the responsible parties. In addition, the **experience** of these parties in performing conversions and/or other real estate experience must be disclosed. The identification of the parties is material because, if there are complaints or lawsuits, those responsible will not be able to hide behind a veil of corporate anonymity.

6.
FINANCING AND LEASE ARRANGEMENTS

The nature of the **Underlying Financing** on the property must be fully disclosed in the section regarding Financing Arrangements. This includes the name of the financing institution as well as the terms of all mortgages — the monthly payment amount, the interest rate, and the maturity date. If there is a land lease on the property, the name of the owner of the land must be disclosed as well as the terms of the lease, including the amount of the monthly payment, any renewal or purchase options, and the maturity date. Normally, the Attorney General's office does not accept land leases for filing if the term is less than 50 years. In addition, the mortgage should have a minimum term of five years.

7.
RIGHTS OF TENANTS IN OCCUPANCY

Tenants who live in a building in the process of conversion to cooperative ownership are normally offered special inducements to purchase their apartments. These tenant rights are **defined by tenant class** — rent controlled, rent stabilized, or uncontrolled free market — and each class is provided with its own unique terms and conditions.

8.
PROPRIETARY LEASE
(applicable only to cooperatives)

1. Rights and obligations of the landlord:
After the date of conversion, the cooperative corporation effectively becomes the landlord/lessor, and the **Board of Directors** represents its interests. The board has the right to set rent (referred to as maintenance), to ascertain the cash requirements of the building, to levy assessments, and to issue additional shares when appropriate. The cooperative corporation is also responsible for maintaining the common areas of the building and common services including elevators, heating, common lighting, hot and cold water, air conditioning (if there is central air conditioning), and the hiring and supervision of building employees. The corporation/lessor is also responsible for maintaining any standard building equipment: gas, steam, and water or other types of pipes or conduits within the walls, ceilings, or floors, as well as air conditioning and heating equipment for the building.

2. Rights and obligations of the tenant-shareholder:
Owners of cooperative apartments are called tenant-shareholders. They have the right to reside in their designated apartment and must pay maintenance on a periodic basis, usually monthly. They may not transfer their interest or sublease their apartment without the consent of the board of directors.

Tenant-shareholders are **responsible for the interior** of their apartments, including the maintenance, repair, and replacement of plumbing, gas, and heating fixtures and appliances. They are also responsible for exposed gas, steam, and water pipes extending from the wall to the fixtures, and any special pipes or equipment they may place in the walls, ceilings, or floors. Tenant-shareholders must also maintain, repair, and replace electrical circuits, fixtures, and appliances running from the junction box at the riser through the apartment, including meters, fuse boxes, and circuit breakers.

9.
BYLAWS

The bylaws are the **basic rules** by which a cooperative corporation or condominium operates. They specify the number of members on the board of directors, the nature of the officers, duties, and the manner in which they are elected. Furthermore, the bylaws define the requirements of the annual shareholders' meeting and the voting rights of each owner. They also set forth the corporate **responsibilities**.

10.
HOUSE RULES

Almost every cooperative or condominium has rules that set forth acceptable **practices and behavior** of owners and guests. These rules cover a broad array of subjects including limitations on pets, permitted times for construction, and behavior and decorum in the common areas.

Qualifying for a Mortgage

Parties lending money for mortgages have two objectives: to earn a return on their investment and to get their money back on time. Guidelines for qualifying for a loan are directed towards protecting lenders against defaults and, when defaults occur, insuring that the invested money can be recouped. These guidelines fall into two fundamental categories — income ratios and debt/equity ratios — each of which must be independently met for a purchaser to qualify for a mortgage.

QUALIFYING RULES

INCOME RATIOS

If a bank made a loan such that repayment ate up 100% of the borrower's yearly income, he or she would certainly default, since there would be no money left to pay for other living expenses. Obviously, no bank would do this. Generally (and there are many exceptions), lenders use as a rough rule that the cost of owning a home — the housing cost — should not exceed 40% of the borrower's income. This is a good guideline in figuring out how much mortgage you would qualify for. Housing cost is defined as follows:

Single-family house: Debt service (regular payment of interest and principal on the borrowed funds), real estate taxes, and adequate property and casualty insurance.

Condominium apartment: Debt service, common charges, and real estate taxes.

Cooperative apartment: Debt service and maintenance charge.

Normally, bank mortgages require that a portion of the original loan amount (principal) be returned with each payment for the duration of the loan. For a variable rate loan or a 30-year fixed rate loan, the monthly payment will completely repay the original amount in 30 years. In the case of a 15-year fixed rate loan, the loan will be entirely repaid in 15 years. Loans with a repayment schedule are called "amortizing loans," and the amount of interest plus the loan repayment portion is called the "debt service payment." A loan that has no principal repayment schedule (i.e., no amortization) is an interest-only loan, called a "standing mortgage." On page 116 you will find a table which gives you the debt service payment per $1,000 for differing rates of interest on a standard 30-year amortizing loan. Using this table, you can figure out how much mortgage a bank would give you for your level of income at the prevailing rate of interest.

In addition to the percentage of income rule, which banks refer to as the "Front End Percentage," banks are also concerned that the borrower's total debt payments (from all sources) not exceed the front end percentage by more than 10%. This is called the "Back End Percentage." Most coop boards also have a "Back End Rule" that total debt payments cannot exceed approximately 33% of total income.

EXAMPLES OF APPLICATION

House:
Myron Jones has an income of $100,000. He purchases a home for $600,000 and applies for a 30 year fixed-rate mortgage of $450,000. The interest rate on the loan is 10%. By looking on page 116, he determines that he will pay $105.36 per $1,000 of loan per year. This equals $47,412 per year ($45,000 interest plus $2,412 principal repayment). In percentage

terms, this is 10% interest plus 0.536% principal amortization. In addition, Mr. Jones must pay real estate taxes on his new home. The last real estate tax bill was $6,000 per year. The bank requires that he insure the house, which will cost approximately $1,000 per year. We can now analyze whether or not Mr. Jones is likely to get his desired mortgage:

Debt Service	$47,412
Real Estate Taxes	6,000
Insurance	1,000
Total Housing Cost	$54,412

This is 54.41% of Mr. Jones' Gross Income, well over the guideline of 40%. Mr. Jones will not qualify for the loan.

Condominium:

Janet Rodriquez is considering buying a condominium. Her Gross Income is $125,000. The price of the apartment is $450,000. She intends to invest $112,500 and obtain a loan for $337,500. The common charge on the condominium is $400 per month, or $4,800 per year. The real estate taxes are $300 per month, or $3,600 per year. The interest rate is 9% on a fixed-rate 30 year amortizing loan. By looking on page 116, she determines she will have a debt repayment cost of $96.60 per thousand of loan per year, or $32,603. Thus, she can figure out her annual housing costs as follows:

Debt Service	$32,603
Common Charges	4,800
Real Estate Taxes	3,600
Total Housing Cost	$41,003

Since her total housing cost is 32.8% of her $125,000 income — below the 40% guideline — Ms. Rodriquez would qualify for this mortgage.

Cooperative apartment:

Mark and Susan Smith have a combined Gross Income of $150,000 and wish to buy a cooperative apartment for $500,000. The minimum cash down payment required by the board of directors of the cooperative corporation is 25%, or $125,000. They have applied for a 30-year amortizing loan at 10% for $375,000. Accordingly, by looking on page 116 they determine that their yearly debt service payment rate would be 10.536%, or $105.36 per year per thousand of loan. This computes to a payment of $39,510 per year. The maintenance charge on the apartment is $1,000 per month, or $12,000 per year. We can calculate the housing cost as follows:

Debt Service	$ 39,510
Maintenance	12,000
Total Housing Costs	$ 51,510

Since the Smiths have a combined Gross Income of $150,000, the percentage of housing cost to Gross Income is 34.34%. The 40% bank guideline will be met. However, most cooperatives have their own carrying cost rules which frequently require that no more than 30% of Gross Income be used for housing costs. The Smiths would probably not be approved by the coop board of directors since they exceed this threshold.

DEBT/EQUITY RATIOS

A lender will want to lend less than 100% of the value of the collateral (the home or apartment) when issuing a mortgage. There are a number of reasons for this:

1. Personal loss: If the borrower invests money along with the lender, the borrower has a greater interest in maintaining the property. If he or she has no investment and things go wrong, the borrower can theoretically abandon the home without taking a loss.

2. Foreclosure costs: When a borrower defaults on a loan and the lender must foreclose, there are costs associated with obtaining control of the property including legal fees, real estate tax arrears (which always take precedence over the defaulted mortgage), and the lost income in unpaid interest after the point of default. The lender needs enough "cushion" in the asset value so that, in the event of a foreclosure, the resale value will pay for all these costs as well as the loan principal.

3. Market risk: Borrowers often default when the economy is bad, which is also a time of declining property values. By requiring that the borrower have a substantial equity investment, the lender has created a cushion. If the value of the property declines, the owners' equity will be wiped out before the lender's invested amount is affected.

4. Distressed sale price: Foreclosure sales are frequently "distress sales," which often results in bargain prices. If borrowers have an investment in the property, the transaction loss is first borne by them, and not by the lender.

While banks will lend up to 80% of the value of an apartment (or 90% through their "deep leverage" programs for which they charge approximately 0.5% more interest), most coop boards allow a maximum debt/equity ratio of 75%/25% (i.e., 75% debt and 25% equity). A higher debt/equity ratio can be used in purchasing a house or a condominium.

EXAMPLE OF DEBT/ EQUITY RATIOS

Bill Arnold is thinking about buying a cooperative apartment for $1,000,000. He has a yearly income of $500,000, but only $100,000 in cash. He would be able to obtain a loan for this apartment, even with his low cash down payment, since it meets the bank's minimum requirement of 10%. However, it is unlikely he will be accepted by the board of directors, since most coops have a minimum cash requirement of 25%.

UNDERSTANDING "HEAVY" LEVERAGE (90% FINANCING TRANSACTIONS)

In the case of a condominium or a house, financing programs offering 90% debt and 10% equity are readily available. Usually, the interest rate on such heavily leveraged loans is approximately 0.5% above the interest rate on conventionally financed condominium mortgages. In reality, these loans are normally a combination of two loans: a conventional 80% loan and a 10% "piggyback" loan. In issuing these packages, the lender normally obtains mortgage insurance from an insurance company for the excess over the

80% conventional ceiling. Therefore, the 10% piggyback is extremely expensive money, as the example below illustrates.

The following is a comparison of two $100,000 loans. One has a conventional 80% debt/equity ratio and a rate of 8%. The other has a 90% heavy leverage, debt/equity ratio and an 8.5% rate:

	80% Conventional	90% Heavy Leverage
Purchase Price	$100,000	$100,000
Mortgage Amount	$ 80,000	$ 90,000
Interest Rate	8%	8.5%
Yearly Cost (see page 116)	$ 7,046	$ 8,305

Difference in interest cost = $1,259

Applicable interest rate on additional $10,000 loan = 12.6%

Therefore, the additional $10,000 costs over 50% more (12.6% vs. 8%) than conventionally borrowed funds.

Recently, banks have begun offering "dual loan programs" through which a first mortgage is issued for 80% of the purchase price and a second, "subordinate" mortgage is issued for an additional 10%. This form of financing is more attractive to borrowers than one "heavy leverage" loan, in that mortgage insurance, which is not tax deductible, is normally not required.

BUYING DOWN THE RATE

A bank makes a profit on a mortgage by charging points and fees when the loan is issued and by the **interest rate spread**, which is the difference between the **retail interest rate**, paid by the borrower, and the **wholesale interest rate** which the bank must pay when the loan is sold in bulk to Wall Street buyers (e.g., if wholesalers demand an 8% rate from the bank, the bank may charge you 9% and keep the difference). The relationship between points and rate is not carved in stone. A borrower can usually lower the interest rate on his or her loan by offering additional up-front points to the bank. The rule of thumb is that a payment of one additional point will result in an interest rate reduction of 0.25%.

For example, Mr. Solomon is taking out a loan for $100,000, which is being offered at 9% interest with one point. He will have to pay $1,000, one point, at the time the loan is issued and will have a yearly debt cost of $9,660 (see chart on page 116). If he increases the amount he pays up-front by three points, to $4,000, the interest rate on his loan will be reduced by 0.75% to 8.25%. His yearly debt payment cost will be lowered to $9,024.

NEGATIVE AMORTIZATION

Some loans provide an option to the buyer to make a monthly debt payment that is less than the current interest charge being levied on the loan. Therefore, the payment is not covering the full cost of the borrowed funds. The difference between the monthly charge that would cover the interest due and the actual monthly payment is then added onto the loan as additional principal. These principal additions are referred to as "negative amortization." Obviously, with the principal increasing, and the interest due on an ever-higher principal amount also increasing, negative amortization can be dangerous; akin to a burning fuse on a financial time bomb.

UNDERSTANDING MORTGAGE ASSOCIATIONS

Historical development:
At the turn of the century, mortgages were provided by local banks which got their funds from their communities and surrounding regions. Unfortunately, this resulted in an uneven distribution of capital. Some regions had ample capital, while others had qualified borrowers unable to obtain loans because of a shortage of bank funds. As a result of this inequitable distribution of money, Congress passed legislation forming a number of mortgage associations under government control and direction. The Federal National Mortgage Association (**Fannie Mae**) was one. The Federal Home Loan Mortgage Corporation (**Freddie Mac**) was another. The purpose of these mortgage associations was to provide single-family home financing nationwide by developing consistent criteria, and by creating a national market for mortgage securities. Today, neither of these associations is government owned and controlled, but both are still vibrant, and remain dominant sources for home loan funds throughout the United States. Fannie Mae is the larger of the two, and constitutes the largest source of home loan funds in the nation.

The Mortgage Markets and Fannie Mae:
Banks issue mortgages which they then sell to Fannie Mae in bulk. Thereafter, Fannie Mae bundles the mortgages into larger packages, and issues Bond Offerings on national markets such as the New York Stock Exchange. These bonds are acquired and traded by insurance companies, pension funds, and investors on a daily basis, in minimum denominations of $1,000.

Banks make a profit through:
1. The **Points** charged when the mortgage is issued to the borrower, and
2. The **Spread** between the rate expected by Fannie Mae in purchasing the debt and the higher interest rate charged by the bank on the individual mortgage.

Fannie Mae limiting criteria:

When purchasing mortgages, Fannie Mae has a number of limiting criteria. The most important limit is the maximum loan amount — $300,700 as of 2002. There are additional limiting criteria which vary from time to time and with the type of property encumbered.

Portfolio Lenders and Jumbo Loans:

For loans in excess of the maximum Fannie Mae amount, **Portfolio Lenders** — large banks, insurance companies, and other financial institutions — provide direct lending programs to borrowers. These financial institutions have their own lending criteria, which are more liberal in the principal loan amount. These larger loans are referred to as **Jumbo Loans**, while Fannie Mae loans are referred to as **Conforming Loans**.

DEBT SERVICE PAYMENT TABLE

The monthly or yearly amount of payment per $1,000 of loan that must be made at varying levels of interest to fully amortize a loan over 30 years

Interest Rate	Per Month	Per Year
4.00%	$ 4.78	$ 57.36
4.25%	$ 4.92	$ 59.04
4.50%	$ 5.07	$ 60.84
4.75%	$ 5.22	$ 62.64
5.00%	$ 5.37	$ 64.44
5.25%	$ 5.33	$ 63.96
5.50%	$ 5.68	$ 68.04
5.75%	$ 5.84	$ 70.08
6.00%	$ 6.00	$ 72.00
6.25%	$ 6.15	$ 73.92
6.50%	$ 6.33	$ 75.96
6.75%	$ 6.49	$ 77.88
7.00%	$ 6.66	$ 79.92
7.25%	$ 6.83	$ 81.96
7.50%	$ 7.06	$ 84.72
7.75%	$ 7.17	$ 86.04
8.00%	$ 7.34	$ 88.08
8.25%	$ 7.52	$ 90.24
8.50%	$ 7.69	$ 92.28
8.75%	$ 7.87	$ 94.44
9.00%	$ 8.05	$ 96.60
9.25%	$ 8.23	$ 98.76
9.50%	$ 8.40	$ 100.92
9.75%	$ 8.60	$ 103.20
10.00%	$ 8.78	$ 105.36
10.25%	$ 8.97	$ 107.64
10.50%	$ 9.15	$ 109.80
10.75%	$ 9.34	$ 112.08
11.00%	$ 9.53	$ 114.36
11.25%	$ 9.72	$ 116.64
11.50%	$ 9.91	$ 118.92
11.75%	$ 10.10	$ 121.20
12.00%	$ 10.29	$ 123.48

Putting Together an Effective Board Packet

GENERAL PURPOSE

After the buyer has signed a contract to purchase a cooperative apartment (or a condominium, if there is a right of first refusal), the next important step is preparing the **board packet**. The purpose of the board packet is to provide a profile of the buyer for the board of directors so they can determine whether or not the buyer meets their criteria for admission to the building.

The key qualifications for admission are rarely put in writing. However, certain evaluation procedures are commonly undertaken. The first thing a board looks for is whether or not the prospective buyer is **financially qualified** to own the apartment. The qualifying rules for a coop are frequently far more rigorous than those of a bank. In addition, the board — consciously or not — always screens a potential neighbor for indications of a troublesome personality. Therefore, **personal references** may carry some weight in the board's decision. Coop boards usually try to form an overall picture of their prospective neighbor in order to reassure themselves that the buyer will enhance the building's congeniality and reputation, and not be a financial detriment or rude neighbor.

DUTIES OF THE BROKER

Under New York State law, a real estate broker earns his or her commission by finding a "ready, willing, and able buyer," and being the "procuring cause in bringing about a meeting of the minds on the material terms of the deal." Even so, the real estate industry generally assumes that the broker's responsibilities also include assisting in the successful conclusion of the transaction. Toward that end, the broker is expected to do the following:

• **Obtain from the buyer and assist in compiling** all documents necessary for completion of the board packet.

• **Monitor, advise, and assist** in the completion of applications and forms.

• **Review and verify** all documents, making sure that they are complete and clerically correct, and that the buyer has made the proper number of copies for distribution to the appropriate board members.

• **Transmit and deliver** the completed board packets to the managing agent in proper form.

• **Follow-up and resolve** with the managing agent any open matters or questions that need to be addressed for the completion of the board packet and interview process.

IMPORTANT THINGS TO REMEMBER IN PREPARING A BOARD PACKET

1. Include a transmittal **cover sheet**.

2. In most cases, particularly in **"image" buildings**, applications should be typed and submitted in folders. At the very least, applications should be printed neatly.

3. Liquid assets should be fully verified. The verifications should be presented in the order they appear on the asset sheet.

4. All **tax returns** (including schedules) should be signed.

5. Contracts should be fully executed.

6. Reference letters should be typed on business stationery if possible.

7. If a **Guarantor** is used, this person must present the same financial disclosure information as the primary applicants.

8. If **two or more persons** are buying the apartment (other than a married couple), each must submit a separate and complete board package.

BOARD CRITERIA FOR QUALIFYING A PROSPECTIVE PURCHASER

In most instances, there are no written rules available to purchasers or brokers about what will or won't be satisfactory to a board. Indeed, the criteria for one buyer might be somewhat different from those required of another. However, some general guidelines, gleaned from experience, may help brokers and buyers define typical issues in given types of buildings.

INCOME

1. An **image building** would prefer that applicants use a much smaller portion of their income for debt and maintenance — 15% at most.
2. A **conservative building** would prefer that applicants use no more than 25% of their Gross Income for debt service and maintenance.
3. An **average building** wants applicants to use no more than 30% of their Gross Income for debt service and maintenance.

As a general rule, think of 30% as your guide, and, in fact, all debt should be limited to 33% of Gross Income.

OTHER IMPORTANT INCOME QUALIFYING CONSIDERATIONS

1. Some buildings do not consider **commissions or bonuses** as reliable income.
2. Applicants who are paid substantially on commission and who don't have a track record in their field for at least two years are not likely to qualify for a mortgage. In evaluating "commission only" applicants, banks and coop boards will take the average of two or three years' earnings as their guide.

3. If an applicant's income is lower than required, he or she should consider obtaining a guarantor, a co-applicant, or a smaller mortgage.

ASSETS

LIQUIDITY

Liquidity consists of cash and assets which can be converted to cash within 90 days. These would include stocks, bonds, treasury bills and notes, IRA accounts, KEOGH accounts, SEPs, annuities, the cash value of life insurance and similar financial instruments.

1. Lenient buildings require liquidity of at least one year's maintenance and debt service after the apartment is purchased.

2. Average buildings expect two to three years' maintenance in liquidity.

3. Conservative buildings look for liquidity equal to the price of the apartment.

4. Image buildings may require liquid assets two to three times the cost of the apartment.

OTHER BALANCE SHEET CONSIDERATIONS

1. If an individual has significant **non-liquid assets**, this may be a material factor in the board's consideration. Such assets would include owning a business; having a trust fund that provides a significant income, but the principal is not available for distribution; and owning assets that are held for investment purposes such as real estate, art, collectibles, or other valuables.

2. In an **image building**, the board will frequently expect the purchaser to have a **net worth** in the millions of dollars.

3. If a purchaser has **income in excess of the required amount**, the board will normally weigh this against a lower-than-desired asset balance.

LIQUIDITY AND ASSET VERIFICATION

The purchaser's obligations are confirmed by a credit report. However, the assets must be verified. You will need to provide the following:

Cash:
Copies of the last two bank statements for checking accounts, savings accounts, money market funds, etc.

Stocks and bonds:
Copies of the broker's monthly statement, or copies of the certificates themselves.

Controlled corporations:
1. A letter from the corporation's accountant stating the gross payment received by the purchaser for the prior year and the estimated payment to be made to the purchaser for the current year.
2. A copy of the corporation's last tax return and the corporation's last financial statement prepared by a Certified Public Accountant.

Accounts and notes receivable:
1. For a note receivable, a copy of the note with the amount and terms of repayment.
2. For an account receivable, a copy of the bill sent to the customer describing the amount due and payment terms.

Real estate:
If there is a mortgage, the credit report will provide proof of ownership by detailing the mortgage encumbrance. However, if there is no mortgage, a copy of the real estate tax bill will suffice. If the purchaser is under contract for the sale of any real estate, the contract and status of any existing contractual contingencies should be submitted. If property is leased, a copy of the lease should be provided.

Art and collectibles:
For art and collectibles of significant value, a current appraisal or a copy of an insurance policy in which these items are identified.

Life insurance — cash value:
A copy of the statement from the insurance company showing the current value of the life insurance.

Retirement funds/IRA/KEOGH/profit sharing plans:
For each retirement program, a copy of the statement from the administrator of the plan showing the current balance.

COOPERATIVE BOARD OF DIRECTORS APPROVAL RIGHTS AND LIMITATIONS

A Cooperative Board has broad rights to reject a prospective applicant. In the case of Levandusky vs. One Fifth Avenue Corp. (75 NY2nd 530, 1990), the New York State Court of Appeals overturned an earlier standard requiring a showing of "reasonableness" and held that the new standard by which a board's decisions will be reviewed is the "Business Judgement Rule." This rule states that the courts will respect decisions made by a board of directors as long as there was no bad faith or fraud. The rule also provides that the court need not evaluate whether the outcome was desirable; only that it was prudent at the time of the decision. The onus is on the plaintiff to prove that proper business judgement was not used.

However, there is one area where the courts are vigorous in protecting the rights of prospective buyers and sellers: discrimination. An array of federal, state and local laws provide protection and redress to a broad number of "protected classes." No board may discriminate on the basis of race, creed, color, national origin, age, disability, sexual orientation, marital status, occupation, roommates, or children living with the occupant.

Federal Income Taxation

Regarding the Ownership and Sale of Residential Real Estate
(adjusted for the Taxpayer Relief Act of 1997)

DISCLAIMER

The following explanation of federal tax rules regarding the ownership and sale of residential real estate is by no means authoritative. Laws in this field are constantly changing and the intricacies can only be adequately understood by an expert. This information is intended to be no more than a guideline and should not be relied upon without the advice of a qualified tax professional.

PRIMARY RESIDENCE

RULES REGARDING THE OWNERSHIP AND SALE OF A PRIMARY RESIDENCE

Home ownership has always received special treatment in the Internal Revenue Code and, in most instances, these benefits are conferred in New York State and City tax codes as well.

Exemption for up to $250,000 in profit ($500,000 for married couples)
If a married couple sells their primary residence, they are able to exclude up to $500,000 in gain on the sale from tax. In the case of an individual, the exemption is $250,000. In order to be eligible for this exemption, the home must have been occupied as a primary residence for at least two of the five years preceding the sale (IRC 121).

EXAMPLE OF THE PROFIT EXEMPTION PROGRAM

John and Sara Thompson bought their first home for $100,000 in 1998. Their neighbor was a movie star who desperately wanted to expand his apartment by buying theirs. They agreed on a price of $600,000, and the deal closed in the year 2000, two years after they purchased the home. Since they are married, the profit exemption ceiling is $500,000. All the gain is tax free. If they decide to buy another home for $600,000, all the gain on that sale will also be tax-free, as long as they sell it for no more than $1,100,000 and own the home for a minimum of two years. The computation of gain is determined on each transaction. There is no limit in the number of times the exemption can be used.

Clarification based on tax law prior to 1997:
Before the 1997 Tax Reform Act, taxpayers selling a primary residence were entitled to "defer gain" on the sale as long as they purchased a new home of equal or greater value within two years. This deferral program would continue through future purchases and sales, as long as new purchases were made within two years of each sale. After the taxpayer turned 55, the old law permitted a once-in-a-lifetime profit exemption of up to $125,000.

In 1997 the law was changed to the profit exemption program described above. However, the new law makes no special provision for continued deferral of "old gains" from prior sales. Accordingly, the gain on a sale is now determined by all the accumulated prior deferrals as well as the gain on the current sale. The one-time profit exemption at age 55 has been completely eliminated (IRC 121).

EXAMPLE OF PROFIT EXEMPTION TREATMENT
COUPLED WITH DEFERRED GAIN TREATMENT FROM
PRE-1997 TAX LAW APPLICATION

Larry and Linda Ginsberg purchased a home in 1960 for $50,000, which they sold in 1970 for $150,000. Six months later they purchased a new home for $150,000. In 1970, the tax law permitted deferral of the $100,000 gain. Thereafter, in 2000, they sold their home for $600,000. Since the gain on the 1970 sale was deferred, it must be added to the gain on the sale in 2000 to determine the total gain. The total profit on the sale is $550,000 ($100,000 from 1970 plus $450,000 in 2000). Up to $500,000 of the profit is exempt from tax. The remaining $50,000 is taxable as a long-term capital gain.

Definition of "tax basis" in the sale of a primary residence:
A profit on the sale of a personal residence qualifies for capital gains treatment, though a loss does not qualify as a capital loss (IRC 165). The tax basis is the **cost of the property** plus the itemized costs defined below:
1. Any permanent improvement which extends or enhances the useful life of the property by more than one year is a **capital improvement** and can be added to the cost of the home for determining its tax basis (IRC 1016).
2. Any **costs incurred in effectuating the purchase** of the home such as title insurance, legal expenses, appraisal fees, lead testing fees, deed recording costs, tax stamps, and transfer fees are not currently deductible but must be added to the property basis (IRC Reg. 1.263(a)-2, 1.1012-1(a)). This does not include costs associated with obtaining a mortgage, which are discussed below.

Any other personal property is treated as a "personal, living or family expense" and is not treated as a capital asset entitled to capital gain recognition (IRC 165(c), 165(f); Reg.1.165-9(a), 1.262-1(b)(4)).

EXAMPLE OF TAX BASIS APPLICATION IN THE
SALE OF A PERSONAL RESIDENCE

Mary Gold is single. She purchased a home for $100,000 in 1990. At that time, she paid a lawyer $1,000 and incurred other transfer costs of $500. In

1994, she made significant improvements to the home costing $75,000, and made sure to maintain adequate records of the cost of these improvements. In addition, Mary purchased furnishings which cost her $50,000. In 1997 she sold her home for $250,000 and the purchaser bought her furnishings as well for $25,000. Therefore, she received a combined total of $275,000.

The tax basis of Ms. Gold's home consists of the original cost of $100,000, the $1,500 in direct costs to effectuate that purchase, and the $75,000 in permanent improvements she made, for a total of $176,500. The furnishings were not permanent improvements, and are not part of the tax basis of the home. Accordingly, the profit on the sale is $73,500. This gain is exempt from tax, because the profit is less than $250,000 and Ms. Gold lived in the home for more than two years.

Tax law provides no cost basis for furnishings during the period of ownership, since furnishings are normally considered a personal, family, or living expense (IRC 262). However, on the date the furnishings were sold, they became "property converted to an asset held for the production of income." The code provides that, in the event of a conversion from asset to income, the basis is the cost or fair market value, whichever is lower. Since the property was sold for $25,000, it is reasonable to assume this represents fair market value. Therefore, the basis (fair market value) and the amount received were each $25,000, resulting in no taxable gain or loss to Ms. Gold.

The example above can be summarized as follows:

Sale Price Of Home	$ 250,000
Less:	
Original Cost	$ 100,000
Fees Added To The Basis	$ 1,500
Improvements	$ 75,000
Total	$ 176,500
Realized Profit	$ 73,500
Profit Exemption On Home Sale	$ 250,000
Amount Of Home Sale Subject To Tax	-0-
Taxable Gain On Furnishings	-0-

The cost of obtaining financing:

"Points" paid to a bank to obtain a mortgage for a primary residence (or qualifying vacation home) are deductible only if they are paid for by separate check at the closing rather than being deducted from the amount given to the purchaser by the bank (IRC Temp Regs. 1.167-10T (j) (2) (1)). These fees are viewed as additional interest on the loan. However, the application, appraisal fees, mortgage recording costs, and other costs involved in obtaining the loan are non-deductible personal expenses (IRC 262).

EXAMPLE OF TAX TREATMENT OF THE COSTS
ASSOCIATED WITH OBTAINING FINANCING

Frank Johnson got a mortgage of $900,000 to purchase a home. He paid an application fee of $250 to the bank and an appraisal fee of $450 to the bank's appraiser. At the closing he paid legal fees of $600 for the bank's attorney and mortgage recording costs of $1,915.50. Therefore, Mr. Johnson's total cost was $3,215.50. None of this was deductible, and none could be added to the tax basis of the property. However, Mr. Johnson also paid the bank $9,000, which represented one point of the loan amount. He paid this by separate check at closing, rather accepting a check for $891,000 from the bank (the $900,000 mortgage less the $9,000 in points). Mr. Johnson is permitted to deduct on his current year tax return the $9,000 as additional interest on his mortgage.

Adjustments to sales price:

The Internal Revenue Code permits a seller to reduce the sales price of a personal residence by the following for tax purposes:

1. All expenses involved in effectuating the transaction including legal fees, broker's commissions, and any costs incurred by the seller in transferring ownership. The gross selling price less these costs is the "amount realized" in the sale. (IRC Reg. 1.263 (a)-2, 1.1012-1(a)).

2. Sellers may also deduct expenses incurred in fixing up the home for sale as long as the work was performed within ninety days preceding the consummation of the contract and payment for the improvements was made within thirty days after the date of the sale. The "amount realized" less these costs is the "adjusted selling price" for tax purposes (IRC 1034 (b) 1-2).

EXAMPLE OF ADJUSTMENTS TO SALES PRICE

Martin Gross wanted to sell his home. He painted the apartment and performed some kitchen cabinetry repair for $2,000 and replaced all the windows for $10,000. He found a buyer who signed a contract to purchase the apartment for $200,000 within 90 days of the work being performed.

At closing, Mr. Gross paid his attorney $1,000 in legal fees, the broker $12,000 in commission, and closing costs of $2,000. The total costs of effectuating the sale were $15,000, so the "amount realized" on the sale was $185,000. He paid the fixing-up expenses within thirty days after the closing and, therefore, was entitled to deduct his $2,000 in fixing-up expenses. The "adjusted selling price" for tax purposes was $183,000.

The $10,000 expended on the windows was not a fixing-up expense. Rather, it was a capital improvement that extended or enhanced the useful life of the property for more than one year. It is added to the tax basis of the home rather than applied against the selling price. The taxable profit on the home is reduced by the $10,000 spent for replacing the windows, without any time restrictions, since it added to the basis of the property. It is important for Mr. Gross to retain all documents verifying the cost and nature of the improvement in order to justify the adjustment to his tax basis if called upon to do so in the future.

Real estate taxes and interest on a primary residence:
Any real estate tax or interest expense associated with a mortgage secured by a primary residence or vacation home is a deductible item in determining taxable income. The interest deduction is limited to interest on a mortgage with a maximum principal of $1,000,000. The deduction for mortgage interest is also available for an equity credit line on a home, but only up to $100,000 of principal (IRC 163,164).

EXAMPLE OF TAX TREATMENT OF REAL ESTATE TAX AND MORTGAGE INTEREST

One year ago, Gordon Honig purchased a cooperative apartment for $150,000. At that time, he obtained a mortgage in the amount of $100,000, which bears interest at 10% and requires a monthly payment in the amount of $878.33, or $10,540 per year. This consists of $10,000 in interest ($100,000 @ 10%) and $540 in amortization (reduction of the principal). His monthly maintenance charge is $500 per month, or $6,000 per year. An accountant's statement of the building's performance showed that 25%, or $1,500 of the maintenance fee, was used to pay interest on the building mortgage, and 25% was used to pay real estate taxes. The remaining 50% was used for operating expenses.

Mr. Honig is allowed to deduct $11,500 for interest (the $10,000 interest on his mortgage plus his $1,500 share of the interest on the building's underlying mortgage). Additionally, Mr. Honig is entitled to a deduction of $1,500 for his allocable share of the real estate taxes paid by the building. There is no deduction permitted for amortization of the mortgage or for the cost of building operations.

Non-deductibility of land leases:

Some cooperative corporations do not own the land on which their building sits, but merely lease it for an extended length of time. These land leases are considered rent for the use of land. No deduction is normally permitted to the homeowner for any payments related to the land lease (IRC 262). There are certain limited cases where this rule does not apply. Specifically, in Battery Park City, many of the properties pay a monthly charge referred to as "PILOT" which stands for "Payment in Lieu of Tax." While this is a land lease, in that possession is for a defined length of time, the IRS has accepted the payment as equivalent to real estate tax and allowed it to be deductible.

Non-deductibility of assessments:

Assessments levied by the cooperative corporation on tenant-shareholders for building improvements are normally not deductible (IRC 262).

Costs Associated with Moving:

Normally moving expenses are not deductible. However, there is an exception when you are moving as a result of a new job that is located at least 50 miles away from your previous one and you stay employed for at least 39 weeks at that job (IRC 217).

INVESTMENT PROPERTY

RULES RELATING TO THE OWNERSHIP OF INVESTMENT PROPERTY

All expenses associated with the operation of business or investment property are normally deductible:
Any expenditure made to cover "ordinary and necessary" operating expenses of an investment property are fully deductible as long as the property is being held with the intent of making a profit. If the payment relates to a service or improvement with a useful life of more than one year it must be "allocated" over that useful period as "amortization" or "depreciation" (IRC 162 (a), 212, 167).

EXAMPLE OF DEDUCTIONS ON A CONDOMINIUM

Martin Sanchez purchased a condominium apartment at the beginning of the year for $180,000. He rented the apartment out for $3,000 per month. His monthly common charge is $300 per month ($3,600 per year), and he has a monthly mortgage payment of $878.33 ($10,000 in interest and $540 in amortization for the year), and a yearly real estate tax bill of $3,000. In addition, Mr. Sanchez paid a real estate broker $5,400 to rent the apartment under a two-year lease and made repairs to the apartment in the amount of $500. When Mr. Sanchez prepares his yearly tax return, the following treatment of these items will occur:

INCOME

Rent $ 36,000
$3,000 per month for 12 months, as defined in the lease.

EXPENSES

Common Charge $ 3,600
Fully deductible as an ordinary and necessary expense.

Real Estate Taxes $ 3,000

Fully deductible as an ordinary and necessary expense.

Repairs $ 500

Fully deductible as an ordinary and necessary expense.

Interest on Mortgage $ 10,000

Fully deductible as investment interest expense.

Principal Amortization —

Not deductible as a return of a loan.

Broker's Fee $ 2,700

Since the fee covers the two years of the lease period, it must be "amortized" over that period: $2,700 in expense in the current year and $2,700 in the subsequent year. Depending upon market conditions, this fee may be paid by the tenant. In that case, it would not be deductible by the owner.

Depreciation $ 6,545

In addition to operating expenses, an owner of investment property is entitled to a depreciation deduction (which is a non-cash expense) that reduces the tax basis of the property. Depreciation is the standard method for recognizing the expiration of the useful life of an asset. The depreciation deduction is based on the original cost of residential real estate, and is spread out over a period of 27.5 years. Accordingly, 1/27.5th of the full tax basis of the depreciable property is deducted each year for 27.5 years (IRC 168 (c)).

EXAMPLE OF DEPRECIATION OF A CONDOMINIUM

Since this is investment property, Martin Sanchez is entitled to take a deduction for depreciation on his condominium unit of 1/27.5th of his original tax basis of $180,000. Therefore, his depreciation deduction is $6,545. Mr. Sanchez must also reduce his tax basis by a comparable amount, to $173,455. In the subsequent year, when he is again entitled to a depreciation deduction of $6,545, he must again apply this against his tax basis, reducing it to $166,910.

When Mr. Sanchez sells the apartment, his profit is the difference between the net selling price and the tax basis. Therefore, if he sells the property at the end of the second year for the same price he initially purchased it — $180,000 — he will have to recognize gain in the amount of $13,090 ($6,455 × 2), which is the amount of accumulated depreciation during the two years of ownership. This depreciation recapture is taxed at a special rate of 25% (see page 136).

Depreciation and tax basis in a cooperative:
Depreciation is permitted for a cooperative apartment that is used for investment, trade, or business. A full deduction is permitted for the maintenance payment as an ordinary and necessary business expense, except for that portion utilized to repay the underlying mortgage principal of the building. The tax basis of a cooperative apartment is the price paid for the shares, plus the apartment's allocable portion of the building's mortgage (IRC 216).

EXAMPLE OF DEDUCTIONS ON A COOPERATIVE UNIT, INCLUDING DEPRECIATION

Dean Morris owns a cooperative apartment in a building which permits owners to rent their units as long as the owner pays a sublet fee equal to 10% of the monthly maintenance charge. He has a tenant who pays rent of $3,000 per month. He purchased the property for $150,000 with $50,000 in cash and a $100,000 mortgage at 10% interest, payable at $878.33 per month. Therefore, in the first year, his interest charge was $10,000, and his amortization of principal was $540. Mr. Morris pays $800 per month in maintenance (or $9,600 per year). He also made repairs in the apartment to fix some faulty plumbing in the amount of $500.

The financial report he received from the cooperative corporation stipulated that $2,000 was Mr. Morris's allocable portion of the building's real estate taxes, and $1,500 was his allocable portion of the building's mortgage interest. In addition, there was a payment of $500 relating to principal amortization on the building's underlying mortgage. His allocable portion of the building's mortgage, based on his fractional ownership interest, was $30,000.

Normally, if this was his primary residence, the real estate tax and mortgage interest would be the only items in maintenance Mr. Morris would be allowed to deduct. However, since this is an investment, he is also entitled to deduct all other costs incurred in operating the building as an ordinary and necessary business expense. The only amount he is not able to deduct is his portion of the amortization of the building's mortgage, $500 for the year. His tax computation would be as follows:

INCOME

Rent $ 36,000

$3,000 per month for 12 months, as defined in the lease.

EXPENSES

Deductible Maintenance Charge $ 9,100

$9,600 in maintenance less $500 in reduction of building mortgage.

Repairs $ 500

Sublet Fee $ 960

10% of maintenance charge (varies by building).

Interest $ 10,000

$10,540 payment, less the $540 associated with principal amortization ($100,000 @ 10%).

Depreciation $ 6,545

$150,000 purchase price for the stock, plus $30,000 underlying mortgage pickup, provides a tax basis for depreciation purposes of $180,000. This amount may be deducted over 27.5 years (1/27.5th per year).

Total Expenses $ 27,105

Taxable Profit $ 8,895

Depreciating Capital Improvements:
In the event that an improvement having a useful life of more than one year is made to a cooperative or a condominium after the initial purchase, the cost of the improvement is added to the tax basis of the property. This amount may also be depreciated, but its useful life must be separately determined (IRC 168).

EXAMPLE OF DEPRECIATION OF AN IMPROVEMENT TO INVESTMENT PROPERTY

Dr. Emersen purchased a condominium for his dental practice for $500,000. After the purchase, he made improvements having a useful life of more than one year including alterations of interior walls, built-ins, painting, and carpeting. He determined that the alterations to the interior walls had a useful life of 10 years and cost him $50,000, and that the built-ins, painting, and carpeting had a useful life of five years and cost him $30,000. The depreciation expenses he would be entitled to deduct on his taxes are as follows:

Original Cost of Condo ($180,000 cost with 27.5-year useful life)	$ 6,545
Wall Alterations ($50,000 cost with 10-year useful life)	$ 5,000
Built-ins, Carpeting and Painting ($30,000 cost with 5-year useful life)	$ 6,000
Total Depreciation Expense	**$ 17,545**

Limitations regarding the deductibility of "passive losses":
A loss on investment real estate is "passive" if real estate is not the investor's primary business. A passive loss on investment real estate may only be offset against alternative income (for example, salary and wages) up to $25,000 if the taxpayer's Adjusted Gross Income is under $150,000. If the adjusted Adjusted Gross Income exceeds this amount, then no loss can be applied against alternative income. However, the loss may be recognized in

future years, either when the property shows a profit or at the time of sale as a deduction against any gain (IRC 469).

EXAMPLE OF PASSIVE LOSS RULES

John Byrnes, an advertising executive, owns a condominium apartment which he rents out for $2,000 per month. He has operating expenses, interest, and depreciation that total $5,000 per month, giving him a total loss for the year of $36,000. Since real estate is not his active business, the loss is a passive loss. However, since he has an Adjusted Gross Income for tax purposes of $120,000, below the limit of $150,000, he is entitled to deduct $25,000 against his alternative income.

Although the excess of $11,000 ($36,000 less $25,000) is not deductible in the current year, it becomes a passive loss carryover. If, in the subsequent year, Mr. Byrnes sells the property and has a profit of $50,000, he is entitled to deduct $11,000 from his profit in reporting capital gains income from the sale.

Limitations resulting from "at risk" rules:

In order to be entitled to a deduction on investment real estate, you must be "at risk" for any indebtedness on the property, or finance the property with institutional or bank financing. Any amounts which are not at risk may not be considered in determining a loss. These rules do not apply to a primary residence (IRC 465).

EXAMPLE OF "AT RISK" RULES

Mary Lou Richardson wanted to purchase a condominium for investment. To improve the terms, the owner of the property agreed to provide $100,000 in "nonrecourse" financing at 10% if Richardson invested $50,000 in cash. Nonrecourse financing means that the seller can only look to the property to satisfy the debt and cannot make a claim against the buyer's personal assets in the case of default. Since this financing would not be carried out in the usual way — through a qualified institution providing mortgages to the public — the nonrecourse quality of the loan precluded it from being considered "at risk." The only money at risk was the $50,000 invested by Ms. Richardson, and "at risk" rule limitations specify that any net losses could only be deducted to the extent of the invested $50,000.

RULES RELATING TO THE SALE OF INVESTMENT PROPERTY

When investment property is sold, gains are normally subject to capital gains tax and any loss is a capital loss.

Capital gains:
A capital gain or loss is the difference between the net sales price and the adjusted tax basis of the property. The Taxpayer Relief Act of 1997 made considerable changes in the capital gains rate, particularly as it relates to real estate. The rules are currently as follows:

• For real estate held for less than one year (short-term), capital gains are taxed at ordinary income tax rates (maximum 38.6%).

• For real estate held for more than one year and less than 18 months (mid-term), capital gains are taxed at 28%.

• For real estate held for more than 18 months (long-term), capital gains are taxed at 20%.

• For real estate purchased after December 31, 2000 and held for at least 5 years, capital gains are taxed at 18%.

• For low-income taxpayers, the capital gains tax is reduced to special lower rates (IRC 1(h)).

Special recapture rules for depreciation:
Real estate used for the production of income or in a trade or business is a depreciable asset. Your primary residence is not depreciable, but that portion of your home used exclusively for business purposes may be depreciated if it qualifies under Internal Revenue Service Regulations (IRC 280a). Currently, this can only be done by allocating a portion of the purchase price attributable to the trade or business and then depreciating this amount over 27.5 years. Improvements of the portion of the property allocated to the trade or business may also be depreciated (IRC 167,168).

If property has been depreciated, the amount of the accumulated depreciation previously taken is subject to a special tax rate of 25% when the property is sold.

EXAMPLE OF RULES RELATING TO CAPITAL GAIN
WHERE DEPRECIATION WAS TAKEN

Brenda Johnson purchased a condominium apartment for investment for $100,000. She rented it out for two years and then sold it for $120,000. Because it was used for the production of income, the property qualified for depreciation, and Ms. Johnson took $3,636 in depreciation each year as a deduction against her rental income. The accumulated depreciation for the two years was $7,272. When the apartment was sold, this sum was taxed at 25%, for a total recapture liability of $1,818.

The long-term capital gains tax rate of 20% applied to the $20,000 profit, since the apartment was held for over 18 months. Thus, Ms. Jones' tax liability was $4,000 on the profit, and $1,818 on the accumulated depreciation, for a total of $5,818.

Capital losses:

A capital loss may be used to offset a capital gain. However, if there is no capital gain, then only $3,000 of the loss can be deducted each year against ordinary income. Any balance must be carried forward to succeeding years (IRC 1211, 1212).

EXAMPLE OF CAPITAL LOSS RULES

Mortimer Stone owned investment property that he sold for a loss of $25,000. Since the property was a capital asset, the loss was a capital loss. Mr. Stone also sold some stock and had a $10,000 capital gain. In preparing his taxes, Stone can net his capital gain against the capital loss to arrive at a net $15,000 loss (a $25,000 loss less a $10,000 gain equals a $15,000 loss). However, he can only apply $3,000 of the capital loss against his ordinary income. The balance of the capital loss, $12,000, must be carried over to the next year and may offset future capital gains as well as ordinary income up to $3,000 each year.

An installment sale permits capital gains to be spread out over a number of years, and permits partial recognition of profits as payments are received over the payment period:

A sale of property on terms providing for payment over more than one year can be considered an *installment sale*. In this case, principal payments can be recognized in the year they are received. The principal received is divided by the percent of profit from the sale (i.e., the ratio of the selling price to the tax basis), and the resulting amount is taxed at the capital gains rate (whereas interest received on the loan is taxed as ordinary income). However, if any portion of the installment indebtedness is converted to cash before the prescribed term, the gain must be recognized on its receipt (IRC 453, Temp Reg. 15A.453-1 (b)(3)(i)).

EXAMPLE OF INSTALLMENT SALES TREATMENT

Michael Strong sought to sell his coop apartment. However, since there were financial problems with the building, it was difficult to find a bank that would provide financing to prospective buyers. Therefore, he agreed to provide financing to his purchaser, Rita Long. The terms were $50,000 in cash and a private mortgage (referred to as a "purchase money mortgage") of $100,000 bearing interest at 8% to be paid in equal installments of principal over the next ten years. Only the principal is dealt with as a capital gain in an installment sale. Generally, interest must be recognized in the year it is received as ordinary income. This loan was personally guaranteed by the purchaser, so it was not subject to the "at risk" limitations (see page 135).

Mr. Strong's tax basis for the property was $75,000, so his profit would be $75,000 (the total sale price of $150,000 less the tax basis), or 50% of the selling price. The sale closed at the beginning of the year, and at the end of the year, Strong prepared the following analysis for his tax return:

Payment received at closing	$50,000
First year payment on mortgage	$10,000
Total cash received on sale	$60,000
Profit percentage on sale	50%
Total capital gain on installment sale, first year	$30,000

In the second year, Mr. Strong received an additional $10,000 installment that was also subject to the 50% profit ratio, so he recognized a capital gain of $5,000. At the end of year two, Strong went to his bank and was able to obtain a loan of $50,000, secured solely by the purchase money mortgage of the installment sale. The $50,000 was deemed a "conversion to cash" and was taxable in the year received.

Phantom gain:

A sale in which the property's tax basis has been depreciated below the amount of mortgage indebtedness can generate "phantom gain," which is taxable in the year of sale. Phantom gain exists when there is profit but no correlating cash receipt (IRC 1001, Regs. 1.1001-2, Crane v Comm'r 331 U.S. 1, Comm'r v Tufts, 461 U.S. 300).

EXAMPLE OF PHANTOM GAIN

Melvin Singer owned a condominium for investment purposes that he purchased for $300,000. He obtained a mortgage that was "interest only" (no reduction of principal) in the amount of $250,000. After ten years of ownership, Mr. Singer had depreciated his property down to an adjusted tax basis of $200,000. However, the interest-only mortgage still remained at its original amount of $250,000.

At the end of the ten years, Mr. Singer sold the property for $275,000. Rather than recognizing a $25,000 loss (the sale price of $275,000 less the purchase price of $300,000), he must show a gain of $75,000 (the difference between the net selling price of $275,000 and the adjusted basis of $200,000). It does not matter that $250,000 must be repaid to the bank, or that the bank loan exceeds the property's basis. Profit or loss on a transaction does not take into account the amount borrowed on the asset. Thus, "phantom gain" occurred, since little or no cash was realized on the sale even though a significant profit must be recognized for tax purposes.

SPECIAL TAX PLANNING TECHNIQUES

TECHNIQUE 1
PROVIDING PRIVATE FINANCING FOR INSTALLMENT SALES

Sometimes the only way to sell a property at a good price is to give the buyer special terms. An installment sale allows you to gear the repayment schedule to the needs of the buyer — spreading out payments over a series of years rather than requiring a lump sum at the time of closing. The seller's gain is recognized only to the extent of the profit on each payment received. The profit is determined by applying the percentage of profit on the sale as a whole to each payment. In addition to spreading out the recognition of gain over a number of years, an installment sale can also be used as a device to convert cash payments from interest income to capital gains (IRC 453) as long as the rate of payment meets minimum "imputed interest" rates specified by the IRS from time to time (IRC 1274).

EXAMPLE OF PRIVATE FINANCING IN AN INSTALLMENT SALE

Robert Baker would like to sell his condominium unit, which he holds for investment, for $500,000. His tax basis is $300,000. A prospective purchaser, Adam Roth, has offered him $400,000, and would like to purchase the property as an investment. Mr. Roth has $100,000 in cash, and plans to obtain a mortgage for $300,000 at 10% interest, so that his monthly payment will be $2,635.

Mr. Baker offers Mr. Roth a deal — a purchase price of $500,000 with $100,000 down and the same monthly payment he would make to the bank, $2,635 per month. Baker has been able to maintain the monthly amount by reducing his interest rate to 7.9%, which is above the minimum imputed interest rate required by the IRS.

The advantage of this transaction to Mr. Baker is that he has an installment sale, so that only a portion of the $100,000 he is to receive at closing will be taxed at the capital gains rate. The remaining balance will be received over a number of years under installment rules. Since the loan is structured so that it has a high proportion of principal (taxed at the capital gains rate) to interest (taxed as ordinary income), Mr. Baker makes more after taxes than if he had sold it for a lesser amount, with a higher rate of interest.

The transaction is also exciting to Roth. He is paying the same cash down and incurring the same monthly cost but, because the price is higher, he will be entitled to a greater depreciation deduction, since the property is being held as an investment.

TECHNIQUE 2
CONTRACT VENDEE SALES

There are times when transferring the title to a property on a given date would have adverse consequences, and yet the buyer and seller are anxious to perform the deal and transfer tax ownership within that time period. A "contract vendee sale" (also known as a "land contract sale" or an "escrow agreement transfer") can resolve this problem. The parties enter into an unconditional agreement to sell the property at a specific price and terms. However, rather than closing within a few months, the contract calls for a closing date further in the future.

During this interim period, possession of the property is given to the purchaser, who accepts the burdens and benefits of ownership. For tax purposes, the date of ownership will be the date of contract and possession, rather than the date of title transfer (I. Fred White T.C. Memo. 1974-69, Leslie G. Kindshi, T.C. Memo. 1979-489, Franklin Estate v. Comm'r 544 F.2nd 1045).

EXAMPLE OF CONTRACT VENDEE SALE

Alice Adams owns a condominium apartment for investment purposes that she purchased for $300,000. She is having trouble selling the apartment because the sponsor owns a significant number of apartments in the building, and banks are resistant to providing financing to buildings with a limited number of owner occupants. Her own mortgage becomes due on the sale of the property, so that if she must privately finance the sale she will immediately owe her bank $200,000 upon closing. She proposes a contract vendee sale according to the following terms to Ken Stevens:

1. A purchase price of $400,000 with a nonrefundable $40,000 cash down payment going to the seller who shall hold these funds as trustee.

2. $360,000 is to be paid to the seller at the date of closing, which shall be in five years.

3. Ken Stevens will take possession 30 days after the contract is signed, and at that time will accept all the burdens and benefits of ownership including paying maintenance, insurance, real estate taxes, and general upkeep.

4. Stevens and Adams agree that the date of transfer for tax purposes is the date of transfer of possession, and that each will record the transfer of ownership as having occurred on that date.

5. Stevens agrees to make payments of $3,600 per month to Adams as interest on an interim loan, as defined in an escrow agreement and secured by the contract.

6. The contract is to be recorded against the property.

For tax purposes, ownership transfers; under state law it does not. Since the mortgage is due on sale, and under state law a sale doesn't occur until there is a transfer of title, the mortgage has not been violated. However, the attorneys for both parties must verify that this transaction does not violate any other conditions expressed in the existing mortgage on the condo.

TECHNIQUE 3
RENTING TO RELATIVES AND GIFTING OWNERSHIP

Parents who buy an apartment for the purpose of renting it to a child are entitled to all the tax advantages of investment ownership, provided that the rental arrangement has the same terms and conditions as if it were rented to an unrelated third party. Therefore, a lease should be signed and monthly rental payments should be made at fair market value.

Parents can, if they so desire, "gift" the apartment to their child by transferring a partial value of the property to him or her each year in an amount not to exceed $11,000 per individual ($22,000 if both parents contribute to the gift). $11,000 is the maximum gift permitted to be given by any one individual to another without being subject to gift tax (except for a lifetime exclusion amount). While this is most commonly done with relations, there is no requirement that the gift be to a family member, and an apartment can be rented and "gifted" to an unrelated party with the same effect. It is important that this gift not be in the form of a rent reduction, which can subject the transaction to alternative rules (J.W. Kelly Estate 63 T.C. 321, Roy D. Barlow Estate 44 T.C. 666).

EXAMPLE OF RENTING TO RELATIVES

George Grossman has decided to purchase a condominium apartment and rent it to his daughter Jane who has just started a job in New York City. He buys an apartment for $155,000 with $55,000 in cash and a mortgage of $100,000. Jane and her father enter into a lease at $1,800 per month, the fair market rent. Mr. Grossman holds the apartment as an investment, recognizing rental income and taking deductions for all ordinary and necessary expenses including depreciation.

At the beginning of the ownership, Mr. Grossman gives his daughter $11,000 in equity value in the condominium. This gift is the maximum he can give without being subject to the gift tax. Since this represents one-fifth of the equity in the apartment, Jane can recognize a one-fifth ownership interest in the property and is entitled to a deduction for that portion of the interest and real estate taxes associated with this partial interest as her primary residence on her tax return.

In the second year, Jane's father gives her another $11,000, and so on, until finally, after the fifth year, Jane has been given an accumulated total of $55,000 in gifts, which equal the full equity value of the property. She now has total ownership. Since her father did not exceed the $11,000 per year gift tax limitation, no gift tax has been incurred. Additionally, since the rental income was consistent with fair market value, all tax deductions, including depreciation, associated with the investment ownership of the property are valid as it may relate to any ownership interest held by the father. Jane's basis for the property is the donor's basis after reduction for depreciation taken by her father. However, since this is her primary residence, Jane is entitled to a $250,000 profit exemption when she sells the property.

TECHNIQUE 4
RENTING WITH AN OPTION TO PURCHASE

Sometimes selling an apartment is difficult because of a buyer's inability to arrange his or her finances, or as a result of economic uncertainty. Renting to a prospective purchaser with an option to buy can be an effective means of maximizing profit and give flexibility to one or both parties. Options can be in the form of a "put," which compels the buyer to purchase, or a "call," which compels the seller to sell. Both can be used together in the same transaction (IRC 1234).

EXAMPLE OF RENT WITH AN OPTION

Steven and Susan Burton sold their primary residence for $250,000 with a $100,000 profit and wanted to purchase a larger apartment to accommodate their growing family. However, in looking at homes for sale, they realized that they could not find anything they liked for under $500,000, $100,000 over their affordable price range. To purchase an apartment at this higher price, they would have to save an additional $25,000 and increase their salaries by at least 10%.

Ronald Silverman had an apartment the Burtons liked, which he was willing to rent for $4,500 per month for two years. Along with the rent, the Golds negotiated an option to purchase the apartment for $550,000 at any time within the two years, giving them time to accumulate the necessary funds and improve their income. It also allowed them to get out of the deal if economic circumstances proved unfavorable. In addition, the cash received from the sale of their previous home could be earning interest helping them accumulate the down payment for the eventual purchase.

Mr. Silverman was equally pleased, since he had a two-year lease at a favorable rent and the potential to sell his apartment at a good price. He was entitled to all the tax benefits of ownership until the option might be exercised. This was a "call" option, since it gave the purchaser the right to force the owner to sell. If Ron Silverman could have compelled the Golds to purchase the apartment for $450,000 at the end of the lease, it would have been a "put."

TECHNIQUE 5
LIKE KIND EXCHANGES

The tax code permits the transfer of "like kind" property without tax effect if the property was held **for business or for the production of income** (i.e., not a primary residence). "Like kind" has been rather broadly construed and would include a condominium, a cooperative apartment, or a single family house.

While this arrangement is most easily understood when it is a simple property transfer between two participants (where the tax code specifically states that there is no tax effect, unlike most barter arrangements), a particularly advantageous, and more complicated, arrangement is a "three-way triangular" exchange. Under this procedure, a buyer purchases a property based on specifications defined by the seller. The purchaser then exchanges this property with the seller in a like kind exchange. The trade need not be simultaneous as long as the overall intent is to perform a like kind exchange. Special consideration must be made for mortgages and any transfer of cash along with the property transfer. This is called "boot," and may result in some tax to the receiving party (IRC 1031, Regs. 1.1031 (a)-1(b), Rev Rule 57-244, 1957-1 C.B. 247, W.D. Haden Co. v Comm'r 165 F.2nd 588, Biggs v. Comm'r 632 F.2nd 1171, Rev. Rule 90-34 1990-1 C.B. 154).

EXAMPLE OF A LIKE KIND EXCHANGE TRANSACTION

Alan Berman has owned a condominium apartment in New York as an investment for 20 years. There is no mortgage on the property and he has deducted a significant amount of depreciation. He would have a substantial gain if it were sold. Mitchell Dunn would like to buy the apartment. Because of the tax consequences, Mr. Berman proposes a like kind exchange with an apartment building he has been eyeing in New Jersey containing six rental apartments.

Mr. Berman works out an all-cash purchase of the apartment building at a price acceptable to Mr. Dunn. Thereafter, Dunn buys the apartment building and exchanges it for the New York condo. The arrangement works favorably for both parties. Alan Berman is able to use the wealth he accumulated by owning the condominium without being obligated to pay a large capital gains tax. Mitchell Dunn is able to obtain a favorable price for the apartment as consideration for entering into the like kind transaction. Berman's adjusted basis is the same as that of the condominium. Dunn's basis is the same as it was for the apartment building. If cash or mortgages were to be involved, however, certain special precautions would have to be considered because of the existence of "boot."

TAX REQUIREMENTS FOR COOPERATIVE CORPORATIONS AND CONDOMINIUM ASSOCIATIONS

REQUIREMENTS FOR A COOPERATIVE CORPORATION

In addition to issuing shares of stock and leases for the apartments owned by the corporation, the Internal Revenue Code (IRC 216) and New York State law (GBL 352eee and 352eeee) have additional criteria that must be met for a cooperative corporation to qualify for the special tax benefits which allow its tenant shareholders to pass through real estate taxes and interest deductions on their personal tax returns. These requirements are as follows:

1. *The corporation must have only one class of stock outstanding.*
While different apartments may be assigned different numbers of shares, each share must have equal rights. If a cooperative corporation provides unique privileges to some stockholders and not to others, there is a second class of stock and the corporation does not qualify. For example, if the cooperative corporation designates certain stock as "preferred" stock, requiring additional payment and offering a dividend, this is a second class of stock and disqualifies the corporation. It doesn't matter that the corporation may have couched the payment as a "bond." If certain stockholders have privileges distinguishable from others, the right of the corporation to pass through tax deductions to the tenant-stockholders will be placed in jeopardy.

2. *Each of the stockholders of the corporation must be entitled solely by reason of ownership of stock in the corporation, to occupy for dwelling purposes a house or an apartment in a building owned or leased by the corporation.*
The right to dwell in the apartment need not mean that the tenant-stockholder actually has to live there. It is sufficient that the tenant-stockholder has a right to dwell that is superior to that of the cooperative corporation. If apartments in the building are occupied by rent-controlled or stabilized

147

tenants who have a legal right to continued occupancy due to local ordinances, the corporation is still qualified as a cooperative corporation. The tenant-shareholder of an occupied, rent-controlled unit has a dwellable right superior to that of the cooperative corporation. Additionally, a doctor who uses an apartment for his or her business is not disqualified since the apartment is dwellable, even though the doctor has decided not to dwell in it.

3. *No stockholder of the corporation may be entitled, either conditionally or unconditionally, to receive any distribution from the corporation not out of earnings and profits of the corporation except on a complete or partial liquidation of the corporation.*

In the event that a cooperative corporation accumulates excess funds, these funds *may* be disbursed to tenant-stockholders directly if they are derived from earnings and profits of the corporation. However, no distribution may be made or disbursed from any other source, unless the corporation intends to partially or completely liquidate itself. According to the Internal Revenue Service, if there is an "overassessment," the excess may be returned to tenant-stockholders in the year of assessment without violating this provision (Rev Rule 56-225, 1956-1 C.B.58). One interpretation of this provision centers on the word "entitled." Since it is rare that any stockholder ever is entitled to a dividend, almost every distribution of any kind would appear acceptable since the board would be resolving to do it rather than compelled to do it under an entitlement arrangement.

4. *Eighty percent or more of the gross income of the corporation must be derived from tenant-stockholders.*

This gross income requirement includes income from tenant-stockholders, maintenance charges, assessments, and any corollary fees and charges used to defray costs such as health club charges, garage charges, maid and secretarial expenses, utilities, and related services (Rev. Rul. 68-387, 1968-2 C.B. 112). It does not include amounts received from commercial rents or income from businesses other than providing housing for the tenant-stockholders.

REQUIREMENTS FOR CONDOMINIUM
TAX-EXEMPT STATUS

Condominiums may be treated as tax-exempt homeowner associations as long as certain criteria are met. These requirements are described in Section 528 of the Internal Revenue Code, and are as follows:

1. *The condominium must be organized and operated to provide for the management, maintenance, and care of association property for the common benefit of all members, and must be organized so as to enhance the beneficial enjoyment of the private residences by their owners (Reg. 1.528-3(a)).*

2. *60% or more of the condominium's gross income for the taxable year must come from membership dues, fees, or assessments received from residential condominium unit owners.*

3. *90% or more of the condominium's expenditures for the taxable year must be for the acquisition, construction, management, maintenance, and care of the condominium property.*

4. *No one shareholder may benefit over others through the distribution of the net earnings of the condominium, other than by acquiring, constructing, or providing management, maintenance, and care of association property, and other than by rebate of excess membership dues, fees, or assessments.*

5. *The condominium must elect exempt status for the taxable year.*

In contrast to the rules which must be met for coops to qualify for deductibility of real estate tax and interest at the homeowner level, electing tax-exempt status as a housing association is not critical to deductibility. Rather, electing the exemption permits the condo to accumulate funds and profits without fear such funds will be subject to tax. In a coop this is rarely a material concern, since depreciation of the corporation's building affords a tax shelter for additional cash flow beyond operating expenses.

PERSONAL TAX

The following is a generic form showing the structure used for personal income tax returns. It is useful for understanding the underlying framework behind tax terminology and application. It is not to be construed as a complete and accurate form for tax filing purposes.

Total cash you received for the year $_____

Less: Changes in Assets, Liabilities and Other Non-Income Items

    Loans you received $_____

    Return of loans you provided $_____

    Insurance proceeds you received on losses where
    you suffered damages, to the extent of the damage

                             $_____

    Gifts you received (which may or may not be
    subject to separate gift tax filings) $_____

            = GROSS INCOME $_____

Less: Tax-Exempt Income

    Tax-exempt income you received, such as tax
    exempt interest or dividends $_____

    Deferred income programs such as IRAs
    or 401Ks $_____

         = GROSS INCOME SUBJECT TO TAX $_____

Less: Deductions for Adjusted Gross Income ("AGI")

    Deductions for business-related expenses $_____

    Deductions for investment-related expenses $_____

         = ADJUSTED GROSS INCOME ("AGI") $_____

Less: Itemized Deductions

Itemized deductions for personal expenses including, in part, the following:

Interest deductions relating to primary and
vacation homes as permitted $_____

Real estate tax deductions on primary and
vacation homes as permitted $_____

Other personal deductions, such as charitable
contributions, medical expense allowances, etc. $_____

State Income Tax liability $_____

Personal exemptions for dependents $_____

= TAXABLE INCOME $_____

x Applicable Tax Rate   _____ %

= TAX BEFORE TAX CREDITS $_____

Less: Tax Credits $_____

= FEDERAL TAX LIABILITY $_____

TAX RATES

2002 FEDERAL INCOME TAX TAX BRACKETS BASED ON 1997 TAXPAYER RELIEF ACT (Adjusted yearly for inflation)

	15% BRACKET ENDS AT	27% BRACKET ENDS AT	30% BRACKET ENDS AT	35% BRACKET ENDS AT	38.6% BRACKET APPLIES TO
Married filing separately	$23,350	$56,425	$85,975	$153,525	over $153,525
Single	$27,950	$67,700	$141,250	$307,050	over $307,050
Head of household	$37,450	$96,700	$156,600	$307,050	over $307,050
Married filing jointly	$46,700	$112,850	$171,950	$307,050	over $307,050

CAPITAL GAINS RATE 20%* (The holding period must be for more than 12 months.)

For Depreciable property, the amount of recaptured depreciation on a sale is taxed at 25%.

*There are exceptions to this rule, e.g., for low income taxpayers in the 15% bracket the rate is 10%, based on the holding period criteria.

TAX RATES

2002 NEW YORK STATE AND NEW YORK CITY TAX RATES FOR RESIDENTS

The following pertains only to upper income increments. In considering the tax effect on home ownership, the upper portion of income is reduced so that this component is the relevant element in considering the tax benefit of home ownership in most cases.

	NEW YORK STATE		NEW YORK CITY		COMBINED
	INCREMENTAL TAX RATE	FOR ALL INCOME OVER	INCREMENTAL TAX RATE	FOR ALL INCOME OVER	UPPER INCREMENTAL TAX RATE
Married, filing separately	6.85%	$ 20,000	3.8276%	$ 50,000	10.6776%
Single	6.85%	$ 20,000	3.8276%	$ 50,000	10.6776%
Head of household	6.85%	$ 30,000	3.8276%	$ 90,000	10.6776%
Married, filing jointly	6.85%	$ 40,000	3.8276%	$ 60,000	10.6776%

New York State and New York City taxes are deductible on federal tax returns. Therefore, the tax rate must be adjusted by taking the applicable rate figure (10.6776%), and multiplying it by one minus the applicable federal tax rate. For example, if a taxpayer had a reported income of $200,000 and was married, filing jointly, the taxpayer's incremental federal rate would be 36%. The state and local tax would therefore be 10.6776% x (1-.35) = 6.94%.

Investing in Cooperative and Condominium Apartments

While most cooperatives and condominiums are owner occupied, there are a significant number of people who acquire these properties for investment. The reasons for doing so include:

1. Participation cost: Few investors can afford to buy an entire building in New York City but purchasing an individual apartment can be an affordable way to invest in the market and can offer similar returns.

2. Management: Managing a building can be extremely time-consuming and complex. By purchasing an apartment, the investor gets to share in the professional management hired by the condominium association or cooperative corporation to handle the affairs of the property. This cost is included in the monthly common charge or maintenance payment.

3. Diversification: Buying individual apartments, rather than a whole building, permits an investor to diversify his or her holdings. For example, an investor could purchase an apartment on the East Side and one in Greenwich Village, or buy a studio as well as a two bedroom apartment. Diversification permits the owner to take advantage of the unique features offered by each segment of the market in order to maximize return. Diversification also permits partial liquidation through the sale of a single apartment, whereas a building is normally sold in its entirety.

4. Appreciation: The New York City market has experienced dramatic appreciation that has been most pronounced in cooperatives and condominiums. Investors can enjoy significant rental income while they watch their asset appreciate over time.

5. Tax advantages: Real estate offers significant tax advantages when compared to alternative investments. It is an appreciating asset which can generate a long-term capital gain, and yet it is a depreciable asset which permits the sheltering of yearly income. Indeed, in certain instances the asset can even provide tax shelter benefits to alternative income.

While the maintenance charge to a homeowner is only partially deductible for tax purposes (real estate taxes and mortgage interest), the investor who rents the same apartment can deduct the entire maintenance as a business or investment expense (except for the small portion that relates to amortization of the underlying mortgage principal). When the property is sold, the gain is taxed at favorable capital gains rates, except for the portion relating to accumulated depreciation. That amount, which has been deducted in prior periods, is subject to a special tax rate of 25%.

TYPES OF INVESTMENTS

The various ways to invest in the New York City apartment market are as follows:

Straight purchase — Condominium:
There is very little that is controversial about the straight purchase of a condominium, as long as the unit deed presents no limitations on the right to rent or sell. Generally, mortgages are readily available to qualified applicants for 75% or more of the purchase price at a rate that is approximately 0.25% to 0.50% above the standard home ownership rate.

Straight purchase — Cooperative:
Purchasing a cooperative apartment for investment can be a challenge; very few properties have no limitations on the right to rent or sell. When board approval is required, the prospective tenants must generally go through an

extensive application process similar to that required of a buyer. The deductions are the same as with a condominium, including the right to take depreciation. One unique feature is the determination of the cost of the property for tax purposes. The price of the cooperative shares and that portion of the underlying building mortgage related to the apartment are added together to create the tax basis. In cases where there is no board approval requirement (which brokers refer to as "condops") the economic advantages are the same as with a condominium.

Unsold shares:

An important element in understanding unsold shares is that rent laws currently in force in New York City (rent control and rent stabilization) afford tenants in occupancy a continuing right to occupy their apartments for as long as they wish (with certain restrictions), and limit rent increases to governmentally-prescribed levels. The sponsor of a conversion who owns unsold shares is the owner of these apartments subject to the tenancies in force and the related legal protections. Since possession is unavailable and the flow of income is restricted, the value of these apartments is substantially less than it would be if they could be rented or sold at market levels. Accordingly, sponsors generally will sell these properties at a substantial discount. Buyers look for returns on their investment through increases in rent (as permitted under law), and by future vacancies in units which can then be re-rented or sold at market rates.

In the course of converting a building to cooperative ownership, many sponsors reserve for themselves special rights on units they hold as unsubscribed shares which permit them to rent and sell these apartments without board approval. In many instances, these unsold share rights are transferrable to third party investors, and an investor acquiring these apartments receives the same rights to rent and sell them without board approval. Financing is generally available at 50% of the purchase price as long as the rental income, less the monthly carrying costs, equals or exceeds approximately 125% of the monthly debt payment.

It is strongly recommended that anyone purchasing unsold shareholder rights consult an attorney regarding the requirements to qualify as a designee of the sponsor, and to confirm that any special rights will truly be transferable to the purchaser.

Occupied apartments:
Apartments that do not have unsold share status, and which are occupied by a legally protected tenant, present a situation similar to that described above except that there are no special rights to re-rent the apartment or to sell the property without board approval. Profit is derived from the government-controlled rent increases and the potential gain on the sale of the apartment when it becomes vacant.

Insider rights:
During a conversion to cooperative or condominium ownership, the sponsor normally will offer the tenants a discount on the purchase price to encourage them to subscribe to purchase their own apartments. This tenant discount has value, and knowledgeable investors can purchase the right to buy the apartment from the tenant in occupancy. Normally, this right is transferred via an assignment agreement, whereby the tenant transfers to the investor his legal position in the apartment, including the right to buy at the discounted price. After the conversion, the investor can resell the apartment at the full market price (referred to as a "flip").

Insider rights are a special situation and are rather speculative. The investor must be well acquainted with the conversion process and retail property values in order to avoid the pitfalls of being caught owning the right to buy an apartment in a building that never converts, or where the plan is amended in a way detrimental to the apartment's value.

METHODS OF VALUATION

There are two methods of defining the value of an apartment for investment — the income approach and the market approach.

Income approach to valuation:
This approach calls for the investor to determine the property's rate of return by taking the rent currently collected, or the perceived market rent in the case of a vacant apartment (as long as it is not subject to rent stabilization controls), and subtracting the common charges and real estate taxes (or maintenance charge in the case of a cooperative) to get the "operating

profit." This is the asset's cash return on investment. The investor should then compare this rate of return to alternative opportunities to select the best investment. The investor can also translate the "operating profit" into a fair value figure by dividing the profit by the investor's accepted rate of return on a real estate asset.

Market approach to valuation:
In the market approach, the investor analyzes the aesthetic qualities of the apartment, as represented by the five "Primary Motivators" of Location, Building, Air, Light, and Space, along with the economic criteria of Price and Monthly Carrying Cost. By performing this analysis, and making a comparison to similar properties, the investor should be able to ascertain fair value.

EXAMPLE OF THE INCOME APPROACH

John Small is considering purchasing a one bedroom condominium. The asking price on the unit is $250,000. It is currently vacant. Mr. Smith estimates the rental value to be $2,500 per month. The monthly carrying charge is $750, and the monthly real estate tax is $250. Therefore, the monthly operating cost is $1,000 and the operating profit is $1,500. John multiplies this by twelve to get a yearly profit figure of $18,000, which he then divides by the asking price of $250,000 to get a cash return on investment of 7.2%. In considering his alternatives, Mr. Small sees this apartment as offering the best rate of return and decides to make an offer. He does not consider the cost of a mortgage because the interest rate will be the same with whatever condominium he may buy. If he were to decide that he wanted a return of 8%, he would divide the $18,000 by .08 to get $225,000 and this would be the offer he would make for the condominium.

EXAMPLE OF THE MARKET APPROACH AND INCOME APPROACH USED TOGETHER

Mary Lerner is considering buying a studio condominium for $150,000. It is located in the midtown area, which she evaluates as a "6" on a scale of "1" to "10," with "10" being best. The building has a doorman and is in reasonable repair, and she considers it a "7." The layout of the apartment is conventional and there are no special amenities. It is located on the fifth floor and faces south to the street, so Ms. Lerner gives it a view rating of "5." The space in the main room is 32 × 12, which she considers large. The monthly carrying charge is $350 and the real estate tax is $150. The rental value on the unit is $1,300 per month. In light of other properties she has seen, the asking price of $150,000 is a little high, and she decides it is worth $140,000.

Ms. Lerner then evaluates the property using the income approach. She deducts the monthly common charge of $350 and real estate taxes of $150 from the projected rent of $1,300 to get an operating profit of $800 per month. She multiplies this by twelve to get a yearly profit of $9,600, which she divides by the $150,000 asking price to get a cash flow rate of return of 6.4%. This is lower than the rate of return she would like to get — 7.0%. So, she divides the operating cash flow by .07, and gets $137,142. Ms. Lerner decides that she will use the lower figure, computed by means of the income approach, for her offer. Had the market value been lower, she might have used that as her guideline.

IDENTIFICATION OF RISKS

Any investment has elements of risk both at the macroeconomic (general) level (i.e., a recession, increases in interest rates, trends in the stock market etc.) and at the microeconomic (specific) level (i.e., refinancing of the building's mortgage, changes in the immediate area, assessments, maintenance increases over inflation etc.). An investor should evaluate both the macro and micro risks of buying any cooperative or condominium apartment so as to minimize the possibility of surprises. Some things to watch out for are:

1. Unusual increase in maintenance or building assessment:
Review the financial statement (including the notes) of the cooperative or condominium carefully. Is the mortgage coming due? Is there an adequate reserve fund? How are the funds being spent? Try to evaluate the risk that an assessment or maintenance increase would reduce your rate of return. If you identify problems, you need not abandon the transaction. Instead, add a discount factor to your computations, and then voice your concerns in negotiating the price with the seller.

2. Balloon mortgage:

It is common for a mortgage on investment property, including loans secured by coop and condominium apartments held for that purpose, to have a term of five to ten years and mature before the loan principal has been fully amortized. The final payment is a large one, including repayment of the remaining principal. This is called a balloon mortgage.

Normally, when these mortgages mature, they are renegotiated at the rates prevailing at the time of renewal. However, the bank has the right to not reissue the loan, or to reissue it at less favorable terms. Investors should look for financing that coincides with the period they expect to hold the property. A long-term mortgage on investment property can usually be obtained, but it will cost more. In most cases, the bank will ask for personal guarantees on the loan.

3. Rental tenancy risk:

The income flow from an apartment held for investment is dependent on the financial capability of the tenant. If the tenant cannot pay the rent, the investor must hire a lawyer to enforce his or her rights, which can be frustrating, unpleasant, and costly. Most investors use a broker to assist them in setting standards that minimize their risk and help them find a qualified tenant. A credit check should be performed and references called. A good rule of thumb is that the tenant should have at least forty times the monthly rent as income. Currently, the brokerage fee for New York City apartment rentals is paid by the prospective tenant; however, when the demand weakens, sometimes the landlord pays the broker.

4. Small vs. large apartments:

Buying several small apartments permits diversification and the flexibility to partially liquidate your investment portfolio by selling one apartment while retaining others. Renters of small apartments, however, have a greater tendency to default, since they generally have less money.

Many investors avoid large apartments since they represent a much larger initial cash outlay and do not allow for as much diversification or flexibility. However, since there is currently a significant shortage of supply, the prices and rents on these apartments have risen dramatically. Additionally, larger apartments attract wealthier renters who pose less of a default risk.

5. Unsold shares and occupied apartments:
When you purchase an occupied apartment or unsold shares, you are hoping that the tenant will move out and you will be able to sell or re-rent the apartment at market rates. My recommendation is that you focus on small apartments such as one bedrooms and studios, which have a higher turnover rate than large ones.

6. Purchasing insider rights:
When negotiating the purchase of insider rights, make sure that you verify the offering plan's estimate of the market value of the apartment. Many offering plans exaggerate this figure. Also, the money should be held in escrow by an attorney until the closing and transfer of title takes place and the tenant leaves the apartment.

RENTING A FURNISHED APARTMENT

Furnished apartments often have transient tenancies, with occupancies running as short as one night and as long as one year. The wear and tear may be considerable and the cost of management significant. Additionally, the condominium association may legitimately restrict the level of rental activity if they view the transient occupancy as inconsistent with the residential nature of the building. Still, the income premium can be substantial and the tax aspects of furnished rentals are favorable. Current regulations permit depreciating personal property in a residential unit over a term of five years from the date it is placed in service. This can greatly enhance the tax shelter of the income flow.

MANAGING THE APARTMENT

When an investor purchases an apartment, the legal obligations that normally exist between a landlord and a tenant now vest with the apartment owner. Such things as painting and keeping the fixtures and appliances in good repair can be a significant undertaking, particularly if the building is old and the apartment is in marginal condition. Many investors seek professional management to deal with the day to day responsibilities. Normally, the cost of unit management runs between $75 to $150 per month. If you don't have the time, it is well worth the money.

Analyzing a Building's Financial Statement

How to analyze the financial performance of a building is one of the greatest sources of confusion for many buyers. Frequently, they fear that something about the building's affairs may be amiss and that the financial statements can provide essential clues. The key to analyzing a financial statement is not to find out if the building is running at a loss (which almost every building is) or has a large underlying mortgage (which many do), but to identify the risk of a future increase in maintenance beyond ordinary adjustments for inflation.

CRITICAL COMPONENTS OF A FINANCIAL REPORT

In analyzing a financial statement you should focus on four critical parts: **The Accountant's Opinion Letter, The Statement of Financial Position (Balance Sheet), The Statement of Income (Statement of Operations),** and **The Notes to The Financial Statement.**

ACCOUNTANT'S OPINION

The accountant's opinion is a letter addressed to the Board of Directors of the Condominium Association or Cooperative Corporation that is found in the front of the financial statement. It should contain the phrase "presents fairly," and there should be no restrictive language such as "subject to" or "except for." Where restrictive language exists, you should read it carefully — it may be important.

If the opinion letter contains the words "compilation" or "review," then the statement has not been audited, and it should be viewed suspiciously. An "audited" statement means that an independent Certified Public Accountant has followed certain independent confirmation procedures in order to verify that the information is correct. In the case of a compilation or review financial statement, these verification procedures have not been performed, or were performed to a lesser degree. As a general rule, particularly in larger buildings (those with over 20 apartments), you should presume that a compilation or review opinion means that there is a problem. Additional investigation, such as reading the minutes of the board of directors meetings, should be performed to ascertain if issues do exist.

In recent years, accountants have been adding a paragraph to their opinion letters regarding the omission of an engineering report which would determine the remaining useful lives of the building's components. Though admirable in theory, this report is rarely done. The reasons include the cost and the deceptive nature of the findings, which frequently imply that the building is substantially obsolete. Such evaluations are likely, for example, to consider an elevator obsolete in fifteen to twenty years when, in truth, elevators are rarely replaced but upgraded over time. These reports are frequently misunderstood, because they give the impression that enormous sums must be spent to replace obsolete assets when, in fact, this is not the case. Managing agents regularly complain that the engineer's interpretation of a building component's useful life does not conform to their actual experience. Therefore, they often discourage coops and condos from undertaking this study, and boards of directors readily agree, particularly in light of the adverse implications to resales. Nevertheless, accountants include that paragraph in a supplemental section of the opinion in order to minimize their professional legal exposure for not having identified material risks associated with the cooperative or condominium.

THE STATEMENT OF FINANCIAL POSITION (BALANCE SHEET)

A balance sheet is a financial snapshot of the cooperative corporation, or condominium association, showing what it owns (**assets**), owes (**liabilities**), and is worth (**net worth, stockholder capital, or equity — assets minus liabilities**) at a specific point in time, usually December 31 of each year. The important components are as follows:

Cash, cash equivalents, and reserve funds:
A building should have enough financial resources to be able to handle contingencies. For a building in reasonable condition, $3,000 per apartment in reserve funds is adequate, although some accounting firms recommend three month's building expenses as more appropriate.

Some buildings maintain large cash balances in operating accounts while others maintain all but minimal balances in investment or money market funds. In order to equalize these variations, your evaluation should include all cash and cash equivalents, both bank accounts and investment accounts. Some buildings have an item in the financial report called "Due from Managing Agent." Normally, this is the building's cash held by the managing agent for the purpose of making current disbursements, and can be counted as cash.

Accounts receivable or tenant arrears:
Generally, the only receivables a cooperative or condominium will identify are from payments due from tenant-shareholders or from commercial tenants. Arrears should not exceed 5% of the total yearly operating revenue.

Accounts payable:
An excessive amount owed to vendors can indicate that the building is having financial trouble. If the Accounts Payable is more than 10% of the yearly maintenance revenue, this should be investigated.

Mortgages:

The mortgage balance is normally found in two parts of the balance sheet. One is the current portion, which is due within one year, and the other is the long-term portion. By combining the two figures, you can determine the full amount of the mortgage outstanding as of the date of the financial statement. The portion of the building's mortgage allocated to each apartment (determined by the percent of the building's shares allocated to that apartment), assuming that the building is "average" and the apartment is "average" for it's category, should be in approximately the following range:

Studio	$30,000	to	$50,000
1 Bedroom	$40,000	to	$75,000
2 Bedroom	$50,000	to	$100,000
3 Bedroom	$75,000	to	$150,000

There are many reasons for variations from these guidelines, and many excellent apartments exceed these criteria. However, in general, a higher mortgage will mean a higher-than-average maintenance charge.

Since a condominium does not have an underlying mortgage, capital improvements cannot be funded by refinancing. Condominium capital improvements are normally made by spending the accumulated reserve or by special assessment.

INCOME STATEMENT (STATEMENT OF OPERATIONS)

The Income Statement shows the flow of activity during a given period, usually one year. It tells what has been earned, what has been spent, and what is left over. In most cooperative buildings, the net income is negative. There is nothing wrong with this, since maintenance charges should be determined just to cover the costs of operations and to build cash reserves. If collected income approximates disbursements, then depreciation (a non-cash "expense") will normally create a negative income figure. If depreciation is added back to net income, you will get an approximation of the positive cash flow received by the building for the year after operating costs. This is the amount added to the building reserve fund. The building's aim is not to generate a profit — which will be subject to tax — but merely to cover operating costs and build adequate reserves. The following is a general guideline for evaluating the expenses of a building as a percentage of yearly maintenance collections:

Mortgage payments	25%
Real estate taxes	25%
Payroll, payroll taxes, and benefits	26%
Other operating expenses	24%

There are many cases, in many excellent buildings, where variations will occur from these guideline figures. Frequently these variations are due to a higher-than-average mortgage balance. A more detailed method for analyzing an income statement is presented below.

NOTES TO THE FINANCIAL STATEMENT

The notes at the end of the financial statement detail and clarify the information presented. Though all notes are important, some deserve special attention.

It is recommended that careful examination be made of the note concerning Mortgages. This note will give the maturity date, the amount of the monthly payment, and any special terms. A near-term mortgage maturity is not necessarily bad. Often, when a building refinances, the monthly payment is significantly reduced because of a lower interest rate or reduced principal payment (amortization).

If the building is on a land lease, it is important to review the note relating to the terms of the lease. Pay careful attention to the maturity date, extensions and options that may exist.

Careful examination should be made to the note relating to the Reserve Fund. Be sure to identify that these funds are in appropriate financial instruments and that there are no lending arrangements in which the coop or condo is borrowing money from the reserve fund. If you see a line item identified as "funds due to/from" it effectively means that the coop or condominium is dipping into the reserve to support operations without actually reducing the stated balance in the reserve fund account. You should also see if there are any "restricted balances" noted in the reserves which are funds that are not readily accessible to the building to use when a need arises. These funds should not be included in determining the available reserves of the building.

It is also recommended that a careful review be made of any note related to Contingent Liabilities and/or Legal Matters. This note would describe any pending lawsuits. Most of the time lawsuits, even ones that sound rather onerous, are covered by the building's insurance policy as long as the claim is made against the coop or condo. If, on the other hand, the coop or the condo is instituting the action, then all legal costs must be borne by the building. This can be an expensive and drawn out undertaking which should be fully understood.

Another note to pay attention to is "Subsequent Events." The accountant is required to report any material change in the building's affairs up until the date that the CPA signs the Accountant's Opinion Letter, even if it is after the date noted on the financial statement. If there is a subsequent event, it should be carefully reviewed.

ANALYZING THE INCOME STATEMENT

This overview should not be construed as a professional evaluation. That can only be performed by an appropriate expert with knowledge of the specific property.

It is useful to compare the expenses of a specific property against a benchmark (a "standard") to establish a level of acceptable or unacceptable performance. In light of the variation in the size of properties, the standard must be expressed as a percentage of revenue. This way, though the actual dollar amounts of the expenditures may vary between large and small buildings, the relationship of a particular expense to income remains comparable. When a property differs from the standard by spending a higher or lower percentage in any expense category, the difference is called a **variance**. A **negative variance** is an expenditure that is greater than the standard percentage (i.e., the building spent more than the standard percentage amount for that expense category). A **positive variance** means the building spent less than the standard percentage in that expense item. That a building's variance on any given item is positive or negative has no meaning in itself. Rather, it is what this variance implies about the building and its finances that is important. There are three ways that a variance could be interpreted:

Negative element: This is a potential problem that signals a possible assessment, increase in monthly charge, or diminishment in the level of service in the building if the problem remains uncorrected.

Neutral element: The variation is probably meaningless to the future cost of ownership, and should not result in a future assessment or increase in monthly charge above inflation.

Positive element: The variation signals a possible lowering of the monthly cost of ownership below any increase due to inflation, or a favorable change in the level of service offered by the building.

THE STANDARD BUILDING

The standard building has 80 units. There is 24-hour doorman service, a live-in superintendent, and two porters. There are two main elevators and a service elevator. The building is 15 stories tall. The heating system uses Number 6 oil. The mortgage is $4,000,000 at 8% interest only for ten years. Common areas on each floor are lit by overhead fixtures using incandescent lighting. The building is on West End Avenue on the West Side of New York City. It fronts West End Avenue and has two sides facing the street. The third side abuts another building, and the fourth side faces an enclosed courtyard. The mix of apartments is 15% studios, 35% one bedrooms, 25% two bedrooms, and 25% three bedrooms. The building was built in the 1920s and has an all-brick exterior. There is no visible disrepair, and the building appears clean throughout.

The following are the costs, expressed as a percentage of normal income, for the standard building:

Expense Category	Standard Percentage
Debt payment (including land lease payments)	25%
Real estate taxes	25%
Payroll, payroll taxes, and benefits	26%
Insurance	3%
Water and sewer	2%
Heating (fuel)	4%
Utilities (common electric and gas)	2%
Management fees	3%
Maintenance and repair	5%
Other administrative and general expenses	2%
Contribution to reserve fund	3%
Total	100%

Before evaluating the income statement of a specific building, I recommend that you personally inspect the property to formulate a general sense of the physical condition of the building. As you analyze the financial information, the picture of what you saw should confirm the figures that you are seeing.

PROCEDURE FOR PERFORMING AN INCOME STATEMENT EVALUATION

Step 1. Write down all the income and expense figures on a sheet of paper and attempt to combine the line items to conform to the categories in the standard. The numbers you need can often be found in an addendum to the report or in the notes to the financial statement.

Step 2. Create the denominator by adding maintenance revenue and other sources of long-term income such as lease income and laundry income. Do not use extraordinary income or items such as sublease fees and transfer fees, since these are nonrecurring items.

Step 3. In the notes to the financial statement, **identify the actual monthly debt payment**, as distinguished from the interest portion of the debt payment. Replace the figure for mortgage interest with the full amount paid for the year in debt service.

Step 4. Add depreciation to the net loss figure. In order to determine the approximate amount of operating cash flow contributed to the reserve fund, add back the amount noted as depreciation to the net loss. Remember, depreciation is an "expense" item for which the building expends no cash. If this figure is negative, it means that the reserve fund is being depleted to support operating expenses.

Step 5. "Normalize" the denominator as required. Each line item constitutes part of the "whole" of all expenses. To the extent that one component of the whole varies significantly from the standard, each other component's percentage is materially affected. In this case, an adjustment must be made to "normalize" any major expense category so that the variation from the standard can have meaning for the other expense items. Normalization creates a rough means of adjusting the denominator to remove the "skew-ing effect" of any significant variation in a single expense category.

There are only three expense items significant enough to require the normalization computation: **debt payment**, **real estate taxes**, and **payroll**. Divide these items by the denominator in order to determine the percent-age variation from standard. If the variance is greater than 10% in one or more categories, the effect of this variation can have a ripple effect on the subsequent analysis and the following steps should be taken:

1) If the figure is *above* the standard, determine the difference in the percentage between the actual figure and the standard. Subtract this amount from 100% and multiply the result by the denominator. This should be used as the new denominator for all subsequent computations.

2) If the figure is *below* the standard, figure out what percent of revenue the actual expense item represents. Get the difference between that num-ber and the standard percentage, and add 100% to the difference. Multiply this amount by the existing denominator, to get the new denominator which should be used for all subsequent computations.

This procedure is referred to as "normalization." A variance of over 10% exists if an item that should be 25% of revenues is less than 22.5% or greater than 27.5% of revenues. It is 10% of the standard expense that is measured, not 10% of the total revenues.

EXAMPLE OF NORMALIZATION

125 East XX Street has gross revenue, after adjusting for nonrecurring income, of $1,000,000 — the denominator. The debt payment on the prop-erty (numerator) is 40% of the adjusted gross revenue (denominator). The standard percentage for debt payment is 25%. This is a variation from the standard of well over 10%, and is significant. The difference is an overage of 15%. Accordingly, the denominator must be adjusted downward using the following procedure:

Standard debt payment	25%
Reported debt payment	40%
Difference	15%
Adjustment factor	100% - 15% = 85%

New Denominator $1,000,000 × 85% = $850,000
Therefore, $850,000 should be used as the denominator for subsequent calculations.

The same analysis is used to determine the variation for payroll, using the new denominator of $850,000. It is determined that Payroll is at 21% of $850,000, while the standard is 26%. This is a significant variation of more than 10% from the standard. Therefore, normalization for this second expense item must be performed as follows:

Standard Payroll	26%
Reported Payroll	21%
Difference	5%
Adjustment factor	100% + 5% = 105%
New Denominator	$850,000 × 105% = $892,500

Using $892,500 as the new denominator, it is determined that the variation between standard real estate taxes and this property's real estate taxes is only 1%. Therefore, no normalization adjustment is required. Accordingly, the denominator used for all other line item expenditures is $892,500.

Step 6. After normalizing the denominator to adjust for variations in the three major expense items, compute the percentage of the new denominator to each other expense item. Then, subtract this amount from the standard to obtain the variance.

Step 7. When any expense is a material variance from the standard, ask your broker to inquire about its cause to determine if it will impact on the future operating performance of the property. It might foretell an increased risk of assessment or a maintenance increase above inflation.

UNDERSTANDING THE MEANING OF VARIANCES TO STANDARD

DEBT PAYMENT
(Including Land Lease Payments)

Definition:
Debt payment is the cooperative corporation's yearly cost to carry the long-term financial obligations of the building, including mortgage interest and amortization and any long-term land rent.

1. If there is a high interest rate, the loan probably hasn't been refinanced due to a restriction on doing so, or a high prepayment penalty. Find out when the mortgage comes due from the notes in the financial statement. It may be that on refinancing, the building will be able to gain additional reserve cash or lower maintenance. Either would be a positive element.

2. If there is a low interest rate, on refinancing, the new mortgage may have a higher payment unless the old mortgage was amortizing and the new loan has a lower initial principal balance. Amortization is the process of repaying part of the principal with each debt payment. Frequently, banks offer 15- or 30- year amortization schedules with maturities of 10 years. The monthly payments will pay off the principal balance fully in 15 or 30 years, but whatever balance remains at the loan's earlier maturity date must be paid in full to the bank. Usually, the lowered principal on refinancing is adequate to compensate for any rise in interest rates with no increase in debt payment, so this is generally a neutral or even a positive element. However, if the interest is low and there is no, or limited amortization, the full principal balance will have to be refinanced at a higher rate of interest. This would be a negative element.

3. A high principal balance is unimportant unless refinancing at the same interest rate will be difficult. This is particularly true if the loan is a "standing" (non-amortizing) mortgage. If the loan is amortizing, this is a neutral element. If the loan is standing, this could be a negative element.

4. A low principal balance means that the building is "equity rich." As a mortgage amortizes, the principal portion of each debt payment goes up, while the interest portion goes down. As a result, the tax deduction for interest on the mortgage lowers with each payment. However, on refinancing, the building can increase its cash reserves without having to increase maintenance, and homeowners will get a higher tax deduction as a result of an increased portion of the new payment being for interest. This could be a positive element.

5. Land Rent means that the landowner has the option to eventually sell the land to the cooperative corporation, adjust the rent when the lease has terminated, or take possession of the land and the building at the end of the lease. A land lease adds an element of risk that should be carefully considered in determining an apartment's value.

The lease, as a long-term obligation, is included under debt payment as a component of cost. Since buyers usually become aware of the existence of a land lease before negotiating a final price, the lease itself is a neutral element since it was already taken into account. However, if the lease term is less than 50 years, it has increasing importance in determining the property's value and future costs. The uncertainty of negotiations with the landowner for extending the lease term or purchasing the land is a negative element until it is resolved.

REAL ESTATE TAXES

Definition:
Real estate taxes are the yearly payment required by the City of New York based on a percentage of the assessed value of the property.

1. Real estate taxes above standard: In new buildings, the assessed value is based on a percentage of the cost of construction. These properties commonly have higher taxes than older properties where the valuation is determined by comparison to other existing properties. Since the real estate tax was known to the buyer at the time the purchase price was negotiated, this variation has already been considered and it is a neutral element when reviewing yearly operating costs.

2. Real estate taxes below standard: It could be that the property has a low assessed value or that the property is covered by one of the City's tax incentive programs, particularly **J-51** or **Section 421A**. These programs offer developers temporary real estate tax reductions to encourage new construction or substantial rehabilitation. Look at the notes of the financial statement to ascertain if the building is covered by one of these programs. If so, determine the phase-in period for full real estate taxation. If the property is a participant in one of these programs then real estate taxes will increase, as will the apartment owner's monthly cost. This could be a negative element.

PAYROLL

Definition:
Payroll is the direct and indirect compensation given to building employees. It includes salary, employer tax obligations, health and welfare payments, employer insurance, union dues, and other costs incurred by the building to retain the services of the employees.

1. Payroll above standard: If a building has less than 80 units and still has full-time doormen, it will have above-standard payroll costs, since each unit will bear a larger responsibility for covering the same cost as a "standard" building. Obviously, a 160-unit building can support twice the staff and not vary from the standard. This variation is ameliorated by larger buildings normally having more lobby men and porters, as well as handymen to make repairs.

However, the ratio of staff to occupants is not always the real issue. Rather, it could be significant overtime. Sometimes buildings use employees to cover labor holes and end up paying more in overtime than if the building had hired additional personnel. Sometimes the problem is that building personnel are working in private apartments and are only able to handle their building responsibilities by working additional hours. In certain buildings there is substantial deferred maintenance and the building regularly uses employees to address these problems, thereby limiting their time available for customarily assigned duties. The net effect of these scenarios is that the building is under-serving the homeowners and overpaying at the same time. High payroll, therefore, is either a neutral or a negative element.

2. Payroll below standard: One might think that the economies of scale in large buildings would cause the cost of personnel per apartment to decline. It rarely does. The technical proficiency of the staff in big buildings is frequently higher, necessitating higher salaries for the superintendent and handymen. Also, there are larger areas to clean and more activity in the lobby to support. Accordingly, even in a large building, a below-standard payroll may indicate that the property is under-serving its homeowners by being understaffed or not having adequately trained personnel in place. A below standard variance could be a neutral or a negative element.

UTILITIES

Definition:
Utilities are electrical and gas charges incurred by the building to support common elements and services.

1. Utilities above standard: Utilities will be high if the building provides central air conditioning as a common service. Most buildings, including the "standard" building, have wall- or window-unit air conditioners that are paid for by homeowners. Utilities will also be high if the building air conditions a large lobby with high ceilings and long hallways. The building will also spend more if there is substantial external lighting and/or fountains. However in these cases usually, a building's electrical use is constant year to year, and accordingly the expense is generally a neutral element.

2. Utilities below standard: Utilities could be below standard if the building is penny-pinching by keeping the hallways and stairwells dim, or if the elevator or some other building system has been out of operation for a period of time. On the other hand, low electrical cost might also be due to the use of lower-cost fluorescent lighting. Therefore, low utility costs could be either a negative or a neutral element.

MAINTENANCE AND REPAIR

Definition:
Maintenance and repair is the cost of keeping the building clean and operating in a manner consistent with homeowner expectations. It includes "contract labor" such as elevator or heating service contracts, brass-maintenance contracts, etc.

1. Maintenance and repair above standard: While high maintenance and repair expenditures might mean that the building is being vigorously maintained, another possibility should also be considered. If building systems are obsolete, and not replaced at the end of their useful lives, the building will have to incur high maintenance and repair costs to keep the equipment operational. This would imply that there may be a need for a future assessment and/or a maintenance increase, when a system becomes too costly to maintain and out of necessity must finally be replaced. This is particularly true if the building has limited reserves. If, when you performed your physical inspection, the building looked unkempt and the maintenance and repair charges are high on the statement, it is reasonable to conclude this possibility. Therefore, maintenance and repair costs over standard could either be a neutral or a negative element.

2. Maintenance and repair below standard: If the building has new systems that are covered under warranty, the level of maintenance and repair may be low. Conversely, the building might be mismanaged and under-cleaned, or items requiring repair might not be properly tended to. If maintenance and repair is under standard, it could be a neutral or a negative element.

SUPPLIES

Definition:
Supplies are the cost of cleaning chemicals, hardware, and related purchases used to insure the clean and orderly operation of the building. It does not include significant equipment purchases, materials used for capital improvements which are treated as assets, and can be found on the balance sheet of the cooperative corporation or condominium association.

1. Supplies above standard: It is not uncommon for the classification "supplies" to be confused — maintenance and repair items are placed in this category, and vice versa. However, in most financial statements, supplies are broken out separately and usually refer to the charges from hardware stores. If the amount is above standard, it may mean that the building is not careful in purchasing or utilizing its supplies and there is significant waste. High supply costs could also mean that the building is using employees to maintain obsolete systems, which would require a high level of hardware purchases. Generally, high supply costs are a neutral or a negative element.

2. Supplies below standard: The building could purchase in bulk to lower the cost of supplies. However, it could also be that the building is undercleaned. This could be a neutral or negative element.

HEATING (FUEL)

Definition:
Heating expense is the cost of the fuel — oil, gas or steam — used to heat the building throughout the year. Oil cost can vary as much as 10%, based on the grade of oil used. Gas prices are similar to oil. Steam is the most expensive form of heating, and costs about twice as much as gas or oil.

1. Heating above standard: Obviously, heating costs can be over standard if steam heat is used, or there are inefficiencies in the heating system. However, the reason could be more subtle. The standard building is of brick construction and is well protected from the elements. A building that has greater exposure to wind, or is closer to water, will cost more to heat, as will a building with large windows and open terraces. Another factor is the weather: colder winters are more expensive than warm ones. In large measure, however, the heating system is unchangeable, so higher than standard heating costs are a neutral element.

2. Heating below standard: The lower cost of heating might be due to an efficient heating system, the nature of the building construction, or a warm winter. However, the heating system may have been inoperable at times, or the temperature in the building maintained at a low level. Therefore, a lower than standard heating cost is a neutral or a negative element.

ADMINISTRATIVE AND OTHER EXPENSES

Definition:
Administrative expenses are the cost of telephones and beepers for employees, stationery supplies, photocopies, postage, and other office costs incurred by the cooperative or condominium that are not covered by the management company. Other expenses are professional and consulting fees, taxes (including franchise taxes), and other charges.

1. Administrative and other expenses above standard: This category will be above standard if the management agreement specifies that the cooperative or condominium shall be responsible for expenses normally borne by the management company, or the building provides non-standard services. For example, some buildings have on-site management personnel. In most cases the cost of the on-site office, as well as the cost of the on-site employees, will be borne by the coop or condo as an additional administrative expense. Some buildings provide a newsletter and actively communicate with all residents on a regular basis. This, too, affects administrative expenses. More often than not, expenses above standard are due to higher levels of service and are a neutral element.

2. Administrative and other expenses below standard: If the bills are not mailed, but are placed under each owner's doorway, or if the management agreement provides that the management company pick up certain expenses not normally included, such as photocopying or postage costs, administrative expenses could be below standard. On the other hand, if the management company is responsible for administrative costs normally borne by the building, the building will normally pay more for this added feature. This will cause administrative expenses to be less, but management fees will be higher. Accordingly, administrative expenses below standard is a neutral or a negative element.

MANAGEMENT FEES

Definition:
The management fee is the cost of professional services to oversee the affairs of the building, including personnel and operational systems. The fee also covers the cost of doing the bookkeeping, including all services associated with receipts, disbursements, reporting, maintenance of files, and corporate records.

1. Management fees above standard: There are three reasons why management fees may be above standard. First, the management fee may be levied by the sponsor of the cooperative (or condominium), who also controls the building's funds. This occurs when the sponsor has significant influence through a large ownership position in the cooperative corporation (or condominium). The New York State Attorney General's Office has sought to minimize such abuses by limiting the right of sponsors to vote their shares to five years after the date of conversion to home ownership.

Second, the management company may have performed services beyond those normally provided. Frequently, management companies oversee major capital improvement projects for a significant additional charge.

Third, the building may have selected a company with a higher fee in the hope of receiving better service.

In each case, the overall amount of the additional charge is usually minimal or limited in duration. Thus, this is a neutral element.

2. Management fees below standard: Sometimes a sponsor managing a converted building charges a very low management fee in order to reduce the maintenance charge so that he may sell apartments more effectively. Once the sponsor leaves this position, the building will have to pay a new manager a much larger fee.

If the managing agent is not the sponsor, the fee might be low because some charges are recognized in other sections of the statement (including administrative and other expenses, and payroll expense). This would be the case if a portion of the employment cost normally paid by the managing agent was paid by the cooperative or condominium directly. Some coops and condos hire the managing agent to perform only the accounting function, and the fee charged is lower because of this lesser service. This might

181

create problems if the building is under-served in essential areas. A management fee below standard could be a neutral or a negative element.

INSURANCE

Definition:
Insurance is the cost of protecting the cooperative corporation or condominium association against calamities affecting the physical plant, liability, employee or fiduciary misconduct, and other identified risks. It does not include employee insurance, which is a fringe benefit associated with payroll.

1. Insurance expense above standard: The amount of insurance needed is a subjective decision. Some boards want extensive coverage for every conceivable risk with minimal deductibles, while others opt for "self insurance" in which the first level of financial risk is borne by the cooperative or condominium. Therefore, a variation from standard does not imply any kind of material problem. Additionally, pricing on insurance can be volatile as a result of factors having nothing to do with the operation of the building. Insurance above standard is generally a neutral element.

2. Insurance expense below standard: Boards are supposed to evaluate insurance on a regular basis, but many do not. Rather, they renew the existing coverage without considering that replacement costs increase over time. If insurance is not revised periodically, the premium will remain low but the coverage will become inadequate.

The insurance expense may also be low because the building is over-reliant on self-insurance. In almost all policies, the first level of risk, the "deductible," is borne by the insured. If the deductible is extremely high, the cost of insurance can be lowered. However, if any calamity affects the building, the cost may be passed on to homeowners in the form of an assessment.

A third reason for low insurance costs could be that the building participates in a bulk insurance program which some management companies provide to their clients. Bulk programs bundle many buildings together as one risk to lower overall costs. This is usually an excellent cost benefit. Therefore, an insurance expense below standard could be a neutral or a negative element.

WATER AND SEWER CHARGES

Definition:
Water and sewer charges are the cost of water service to the property.

1. Water and sewer charges above standard: New York City has required, in most instances, that residential properties use water meters. Therefore, the cost of this service is a function of water use. A building could have high water and sewer costs if the number of water fixtures in the building is above average. This could be likely if the building has a higher number of large apartments than the standard building. This is a neutral element.

2. Water and sewer charges below standard: Normally, low water and sewer expenses are due to a fewer water fixtures than in the standard building. This would imply an apartment mix weighed toward smaller apartments. This is a neutral element.

CONTRIBUTION TO THE RESERVE FUND

Definition:
Adding the depreciation expense (not a cash cost) to the net gain or loss gives the approximate amount of cash available to the building after operating expenses. This remaining cash normally accumulates in the reserve fund, and is available for capital improvements and contingencies.

1. Contribution to the reserve fund above standard: It is appropriate, if not essential, that a building make a greater-than-standard contribution to the reserve fund if there is a proposed capital project, an uninsured contingent liability, or a high level of deferred maintenance. However, it may be inappropriate to make a high reserve fund contribution if the building already has a substantial balance and the board is augmenting reserves for no specific purpose. In any case, a high reserve fund contribution is normally a positive element.

2. Contribution to the reserve fund below standard: It would only be appropriate for a building to make a lower-than-standard reserve fund contribution if the building already has excess reserve savings, and there is no reason to further augment them. In all other cases, a deficient contribution means that the building is not creating an adequate base of funds to handle unexpected contingencies or capital upgrades. A less-than-standard reserve fund contribution could be a negative element.

SIZING UP A BUILDING'S FINANCIAL POSITION

After evaluating the operating costs for a specific building against the standard, you should be able to draw an overall conclusion. Normally, one or two glaring issues or a number of interrelated variances reveal critical information about the building's overall financial health. For example, if a building is in weak economic condition you might see negative variances in materials, supplies and maintenance expenses coupled with an overage in payroll costs. This may mean that the building is charging too little for monthly maintenance, and will result in significant pressure to raise additional revenue from homeowners.

When a building is over-mortgaged, a coop will often seek to keep monthly maintenance costs at market levels by reducing services or deferring normal improvements. This is not a good long-term solution and eventually necessitates substantial assessments to cure building ailments that were previously ignored.

I propose that you keep your eye on the big picture rather than any specific variation. Explore what a variation may mean in terms of future dollar outlays or potential reductions in service. In most instances, the risk you identified is already in your price. For example, you're going to pay less for a building that looks old and tired rather than new and pristine. If you see evidence of what you know in the financial statement, don't be surprised.

Strategies for Selling an Apartment

DECIDING TO SELL YOUR HOME

Selling a home is rarely just an investment decision; it is also a lifestyle decision. You are leaving your old world and entering a new one. The new world may be very different from your former one. It may include a change in your marital status, or the formation of a family. Whatever the case, deciding to sell a home is not merely about money. It is also about your new needs.

Two components will determine how much you can spend on a new home: **Equity Capital** (the non-borrowed cash you can obtain to purchase a new home) and **Gross Income**. These are the two figures the banks rely on to determine the amount of mortgage they will lend. The combined sum of your equity and your mortgage principal is the total amount you can offer for your next purchase.

Your other big consideration is why you need to sell. Clearly identify the issue motivating you, and translate it into a specific type of apartment that meets your new needs. Determine the number of bedrooms, location, type of building and services, layout, elements of light and view, and amount of space that you require. Then, check the local newspaper and various internet sites to discover the approximate cost of this type of property. Try to identify at least three or four apartments that might qualify as viable alternatives. As you evaluate what is available, you will become aware of the price and quality trade-offs in the marketplace. This is the starting place when you are thinking about selling your home. It is not defining how much money you want for your apartment, but figuring out where you will go after you sell it and how much your new home will cost.

It is important to include a "cushion factor" in your computations. I recommend that you maintain at least six months carrying cost for both the old and new apartments as a reserve. If you cannot accumulate this, I recommend that you sell first and rent an apartment while you have money, and then carefully explore your choices. The last thing you want is to have your sale fall through while you are on contract to buy. This could put you in an economic squeeze. Also, coop boards will look for at least one to two years maintenance in liquid assets while evaluating your financial ability to carry the new home. Brokers frequently recommend a cushion factor equal to 10% of the purchase price of an apartment to their buyers.

DETERMINING THE VALUE OF YOUR APARTMENT

Compare your apartment to other apartments with similar qualities that have sold, or are for sale, in your building and in your surrounding neighborhood, and then adjust upward or downward for your apartment's particular amenities and maintenance charge. Review the classified section of the newspaper and internet sites to find comparable apartments. All of this can be helpful in forming a preliminary impression of the value of your home.

CREATING A STRATEGY FOR SELLING

When you have decided to sell, you should call several real estate brokers to get their estimates of the value of your apartment and learn how they would serve your interests if they represented you in the sale. Real estate brokers can provide a number of invaluable services, including:

Confirming your valuation:
While you should develop your own sense of the market, it is important to get a broker's confirmation — or a response to the contrary. Either way, he or she should not merely estimate your apartment's value, but also should provide substantive support for that valuation based on his or her knowledge of the market.

Defining the state of the market:
It is useful to understand the current relationship between supply and demand. A limited supply of listings implies a strong selling position; a large supply of apartments implies weakening prices.

Developing a marketing strategy:
Ask the broker how he or she will attempt to sell your property, including how and where your apartment will be advertised. Ask if he or she plans to host an open house and, if so, how frequently.

Other services:
A broker should be able to explain the entire selling process and tell you how he or she will actively participate. Their plan should include finding qualified buyers, negotiating a deal on terms acceptable to you, assisting the buyer in getting a mortgage, insuring that any board application material is properly compiled in a timely fashion, and generally monitoring the transaction as it moves towards completion.

SELECTING A BROKER

First and foremost, a good broker should be someone you like and believe in. He or she should be knowledgeable about the market, acquainted with the kinds of issues you have, and be able to attract the greatest number of qualified buyers. The ideal broker has good verbal skills and is persuasive. Also, you want someone who respects how important this transaction is to you, and who is accommodating and flexible. When you invite brokers to your home, listen carefully. At the first meeting, what they say to you is more important than what you say to them. You are interviewing them to find the person who will most effectively represent your interests. The person you select is your agent; you are his or her principal.

ENTERING INTO AN EXCLUSIVE AGREEMENT TO SELL YOUR HOME

Normally, a broker will want you to sign an exclusive agreement giving him or her the sole right to sell your apartment. This agreement comes in two forms: an **exclusive right to sell** and an **exclusive agency**. The "right to sell" agreement provides that when your home is sold, a commission is owed to the broker, whatever the circumstances of the sale. The "exclusive agency" agreement provides that the broker is your sole representative in selling the apartment. On the sale, he or she will be entitled to a commission, unless the sale is made directly by you without the participation of any broker or agent.

Obviously, brokers prefer the broader protection of the right to sell agreement, since it eliminates potential misunderstandings and provides greater assurance that his or her efforts to sell the property will eventually be compensated. However, the exclusive agency agreement is appropriate if you intend to try to make a sale yourself. If so, you will want to have your efforts acknowledged and confirmed up front, apart from the broker's arrangements for selling the property.

PROMOTING YOUR APARTMENT FOR SALE

CO-BROKERING

The first fundamental principle for marketing your apartment is to "get the word out." The probability of generating interest and offers is greatest when all potential buyers are exposed to the listing. Therefore, the exclusive broker should aggressively distribute the listing to a large number of brokerage firms on a shared-commission basis.

Some brokers believe it is best to minimize exposure of the property to other brokers because they fear that overexposure will diminish buyer enthusiasm. This is not true. In the residential market there is an active rotation of buyers, so all properties are evaluated on a regular basis by a new population. Regardless of which broker a seller selects, there are serious buyers working with many different brokerage firms, and these qualified candidates are unlikely to find out about your property unless your broker gets the information to their broker. Therefore, every effort should be made to insure broad distribution of your listing throughout the local marketplace.

SELECTING ADVERTISING MEDIA

A second fundamental concept is the "thirsty animal principle." This premise states that when an animal is thirsty it looks for water in the most likely place. In other words, when buyers want to purchase homes, they look at the media sources most likely to advertise the kind of homes they desire. High-circulation media are preferable to those with low circulation. Targeted media, which focus on displaying homes for sale, are superior to those with a more general orientation. Your exclusive agent should know this, and should target his or her marketing efforts to media which offer the best potential response. A seller should not be satisfied merely because his or her apartment has been advertised; *where* it is advertised is far more important.

Some brokers issue in-house magazines and flyers to promote their properties. These are of minimal value unless they are broadly distributed as inserts in high-circulation newspapers or by an extensive direct-mail campaign. Issuing this promotional material at the broker's office or on a selective basis does little to assist in the sale of your property. Don't be impressed by glossy brochures; ask how the brochures are being distributed. A good-looking marketing piece is only valuable when seen by a large population of prospective buyers.

TARGETING YOUR AUDIENCE

A third fundamental principle, "aiming at the target," relates to the advertisement itself. If you go hunting in the forest and see a target, you stand a better chance of hitting something if you aim at the target rather than at the forest. You might hit something if you aim at the forest, but your chances are not as good.

Look at the advertisement your exclusive agent uses to promote your apartment. Is it promoting your apartment, or is it promoting the brokerage firm? Are they aiming at the target, or the forest? If the ad promotes the brokerage firm, buyers for your apartment are not the primary target.

CREATING SALES APPEAL

A fourth fundamental principle is that an advertisement that looks attractive and is well written creates more attention than one that isn't. The exclusive agent should write ads that emphasize the best qualities of your apartment. If the ad is a classified advertisement, it should place the important attributes in the beginning of the text, without superfluous adjectives. If a display ad is used, an appealing picture is desirable. The ad should not be cluttered.

MULTIPLE LISTING SYSTEMS IN NEW YORK CITY

In most areas of the country, local brokers have formed associations in order to create a central clearing system for the dissemination of information about apartments for sale. This system, normally referred to as a Multiple Listing System ("MLS") does exist in certain areas of New York City and a seller should insist that their apartment be placed on the MLS as a condition to an exclusive agreement. However, in other parts of the City, including Manhattan, MLS does not exist and brokers normally utilize E-Mail and faxes to disseminate information to other firms. Where MLS does not exist, a seller should make sure that the broker expressly affirms his/her intention to share the listing with other brokerage companies and provides a list of those other firms which will be contacted. You should review that list in order to make sure that it is complete and if any companies are missing which you know handle your area, insist that they be added.

ATTRIBUTES OF A GOOD REAL ESTATE BROKERAGE COMPANY

Specialization:
A good real estate brokerage company will be a specialist in your market. Brokers who handle many different kinds of properties usually have less expertise than those who serve specific niches. Your broker should be well-acquainted with the neighborhood in which the apartment is located, which is best evidenced by the company having an office there. Brokers with local offices are better informed, and can better educate the seller. They also can present a broader array of properties for sale in their neighborhood, thus attracting buyers.

Trained sales force:
Training is fundamental in order to provide the highest quality service. A brokerage company that emphasizes training will have a more effective sales force. At the very least, each salesperson should be well-versed in the standard form contract, preparing a board packet, selling techniques and negotiating strategies.

Computerization:
Given the current demands of the marketplace, a brokerage company cannot be efficient without technology. An effective real estate brokerage company must use a computerized listing system and have an internet site.

The Challenges in Selling an Apartment

SELLING AN APARTMENT WITH A HIGH MAINTENANCE

While a seller will want the highest possible price for his or her apartment, a buyer will attempt to buy at the lowest cost. The terms "price" and "cost" are not synonymous. The price-conscious seller is looking at the amount of money to be received at closing, while the cost-conscious buyer is looking at the amount of cash that must be invested and how much it will cost to carry the apartment via maintenance charge and monthly debt payment.

In evaluating cost, a high maintenance augments the cost of carrying an apartment. Therefore, a buyer will seek to reduce the purchase price to bring the cost in line with other properties. The appropriate price reduction is calculated by treating the excess over normal maintenance as equivalent to monthly debt service on an additional borrowing. This excess amount should then be used to compute the necessary debt principal that would be required to generate an interest payment equivalent to the maintenance overage. Thereafter, the price of the apartment should be reduced by removing that additional borrowing from the purchase price.

For example, an apartment has a price of $300,000, which is deemed to be the fair market value of the apartment assuming it had an average maintenance. However, the apartment has a maintenance of $2,000 per month, which is deemed to be $500 per month, or $6,000 per year, over the average maintenance charge for comparable apartments. The long-term cost of borrowing money is 10%. Therefore, the computed borrowing value of this excess is $60,000, determined by dividing the excess cost per year by the long-term interest rate. According to this theoretical model, the purchase price should be adjusted downward to $240,000 to reflect the excess maintenance.

While the theoretical model appears logical, it occasionally results in a price significantly below what a seller is willing to accept. In this case, market forces predominate to create the appropriate price adjustment. The following strategies can be used to find a compromise:

• *The seller can provide a supplemental fund to support the maintenance for a limited time, such as five years.*
• *The seller can pay for a "buy down" of the buyer's mortgage rate. Most banks have buy-down programs which permit, for a defined charge, a reduced interest rate and reduced monthly payment on the buyer's mortgage.*

SELLING AN APARTMENT IN A BUILDING WITHOUT AN ADEQUATE RESERVE FUND

Buyers are often cautious about purchasing an apartment in a building that has an inadequate reserve fund. An acceptable reserve fund is defined by many brokers as $3,000 per apartment as long as there are no material adverse conditions in the building. Unfortunately, many buildings with inadequate reserve funds also tend to have substantial deferred maintenance, and are resistant to levying assessments against tenant-shareholders adequate enough to improve conditions, except in dire circumstances. The risk of an assessment or increase in maintenance is, accordingly, difficult to determine.

One strategy is to look at the financial statements of three comparable buildings in the area, and figure out the average allocated reserve fund for an apartment similar to the one under consideration. You can propose to give the buyer a separate supplemental payment equal to the difference between this amount and the reserve fund allocated to your apartment in compensation for a projected future assessment. Your broker should assist you in obtaining these figures and computing these costs.

Another point to consider is to advise the buyer that the price of the apartment if the building were in pristine condition would be greater than the current asking price and implied in this lower price is a discount for the current condition of the building and the uncertainty about future assessments. Therefore, the only sum that should realistically be allocated to reserve is the amount at standard which is $3,000.

SELLING A SMALL APARTMENT

No apartment is small, except by comparison to other properties in the marketplace. All apartments are evaluated on the basis of their comparable attributes, and a smaller property may have positive features which ameliorate that one negative aspect. The following strategies can be useful:

- *Paint the apartment white.*
- *Explain "how the apartment works," giving suggestions like built-ins, sofa beds, and leaf tables.*
- *Emphasize that it is bigger than a hotel room, and much less expensive.*
- *Define the economic cost of the extra footage.*
- *Compare the cost of ownership on an after-tax basis to the rent alternative (see Rent vs. Buy Analysis on page 46).*
- *Emphasize the apartment's positive attributes, such as the quality of the location, the building's services, the amount of light, or the attractive view.*

SELLING A DARK APARTMENT

To sell a dark apartment, you must remove any sense of dreariness. An effective window treatment can distract the eye from lack of light, and artificial lighting around the window can be effective to add a dimension of comfort. You should also point out the significant price benefit over a similar apartment with light, and emphasize the apartment's favorable attributes, such as desirable location, building services, or size.

WHAT TO DO WHEN YOU FIND THE RIGHT APARTMENT AND YOU HAVEN'T SOLD YOUR HOME

When you find the apartment you want to buy and have not yet sold the apartment you own, you risk owning two apartments at the same time and having more expenses than you are capable of handling. One way of dealing with this is to determine how much excess cost you would have to carry over six months because of the additional apartment. Reduce your asking price for your current apartment by this amount. This should generate a number of bids by highly qualified, committed buyers. Since you are selling at a discount, you can demand a closing date that closely correlates to the closing date for your purchase.

Another alternative is to arrange for a bridge loan from a bank in order to close on your purchase and carry both properties. The bridge loan proceeds will support your added expenses for a while, but you will probably have to pay points as well as a higher than normal interest rate for the loan.

A third choice is to forget about your purchase and recognize that you can always find an apartment you like. A later purchase may cost a little more, but the reduction in risk may be worth the money.

WHAT TO DO WHEN YOU HAVE TO SELL YOUR APARTMENT AT A LOSS

If you sell your home at a loss, this loss is not tax deductible. Many people falsely believe they can create tax recognition for a loss by converting the property to investment property through renting it, and then selling it later. They believe that since it was investment property when sold, the loss can be designated as an investment loss rather than a loss on the sale of a primary residence. However, this is not how the tax law works. At the time of conversion to an investment, you must reduce the valuation of the asset to its fair market value. Therefore, the loss you have already realized is not converted to an investment loss and remains unrecognizable.

However, conversion to investment use is still a good idea in certain circumstances — particularly if the home's value has declined to below the remaining mortgage. Selling in this case would be problematic, since the owner would have to pay the bank more than he or she would receive from the buyer at closing. In this case, it pays to consider converting the property to an investment by renting it at fair market value. The rental income should cover the carrying cost of the home, and possibly even offer the owner a profit. Depreciation may be taken on investment property, so any profits will probably be tax free. Often, owners have converted primary residences to investment use and found the profits to be so substantial, that even when prices rose again they had little interest in selling. It is also important to note that the additional income generated from the property, when added to your other earnings, may improve your creditworthiness and help you get another mortgage on a subsequent home.

WHAT TO DO WHEN THE BUYER WANTS CONCESSIONS AFTER THE CONTRACT IS SIGNED

Once a contract is signed, both the seller and buyer have the right to compel performance under the terms of the contract. Indeed, the standard contract clearly states that the seller has the right to take possession of the 10% contract deposit as liquidating damages if the buyer fails to perform under his or her specified obligations.

However, there are times when the buyer will assert a breach of terms by the seller and will seek concessions based on those violations. In this case, it is not clear that the buyer's deposit is available as liquidating damages, and the buyer may have a legitimate right to insist that a problem either be rectified or that there be a price concession commensurate with the damage caused. An unresolved dispute can hurt both parties because it could lead to expensive litigation. The seller should consider making concessions if he or she has misrepresented the amount of maintenance; if there has been an assessment not identified in the contract; or if there has been damage to the property. Some ways a seller can handle such problems are:

• **For an error in the reported maintenance:** *Calculate the difference between the old and new maintenance charges and multiply by 12. The ration-*

ale you can use is that buildings frequently make annual adjustments for maintenance, and you are willing to pay the increased cost until the next adjustment period.

• **For an unidentified assessment:** If the assessment is for a capital improvement, take the position that the assessment improves the value of the property and therefore warrants no adjustment. If the buyer disputes this position, negotiate to share the assessment equally.

• **For damage to the apartment:** Bring in a contractor and get a bid for the repair. Tell the buyer that you will make a concession to the extent of the cost of the repair, based on the contractor's estimate.

• **For unforeseen change in circumstances of the buyer:** If the buyer wants a concession because he or she cannot get the money required to close the deal, you can either consider issuing a one-year personal note for the open balance at a high rate of interest, or put the apartment back on the market, keeping the buyer's deposit as liquidating damages.

• **For when market prices have declined and the buyer wants a concession in light of the apartment's lowered value:** Consider what you could conservatively sell the apartment for if the buyer abandons the deal, and add to that the 10% contract deposit you could keep as damages. If that figure is less than the buyer is willing to pay, you should lower your price as a concession.

WHAT TO DO WHEN YOU GET AN OFFER RIGHT AFTER YOU PLACE THE APARTMENT ON THE MARKET

It is very common for a seller to receive substantial interest in his or her apartment soon after the property is listed for sale. All the salespeople who are informed about the new offering will search their buyer inventories to see if there are any viable candidates and, if there are, will quickly arrange appointments. Many of these buyers have already had considerable experience in the market, and are ready to enter a bid after a single viewing. Some sellers misconstrue this initial flurry of activity as indicative of general market interest, so they tend to resist early offers. However, when the dust settles and these initial offers fade away, the seller must deal with the next round of buyers, many of whom have less experience and are reluctant to make offers without carefully exploring all the possible alternatives. The level of activity lessens, and offers become more sparse.

It is my recommendation that you value your apartment carefully before you put it on the market. Then, when the right offer appears, take it and be happy. If you have reservations about an early offer and you're not sure it's worth taking, direct your broker to call a number of other brokerage firms to tell them you are about to accept an offer. If they have any prospective buyers who may be interested in beating the existing bid they will tell your broker. Remember, "a bird in hand is worth two in the bush."

WHAT TO DO IF YOU CHANGE YOUR MIND AFTER YOU AGREE TO SELL YOUR APARTMENT TO A SPECIFIC BUYER AT A SPECIFIC PRICE

There are real risks in changing your mind after you have agreed to an offer. One issue is your broker. Under New York State law, a broker is entitled to a commission after he or she finds a "ready, willing, and able buyer" and is the "procuring cause" in bringing about a "meeting of the minds on the material terms of the deal." There is no requirement that such an agreement be in writing, and reneging on the acceptance of an offer can still leave you with the obligation to pay your broker a commission.

The best way to handle this issue is to enter into an exclusive agreement with a broker that stipulates a commission is only due if a contract is signed, and subsequently closes. This will effectively protect you from any broker claims.

In dealing with the buyer, New York State law stipulates that a valid agreement for the sale of real estate must be in writing. If you have not signed a contract, you are free to change your mind. However, if a contract has already been signed and you have changed your mind, you can ask the buyer to relinquish his or her position and offer to make a payment to cover his or her "costs." Depending on the offered settlement, you may get the buyer to accommodate you.

If you enter into one agreement to sell your home, and another one to buy a new home, only to have the "buy" agreement fail, you remain obligated to sell your home. In this case, you should quickly look for another purchase, obtain a short-term rental, or renegotiate the price and terms to resurrect the purchase that fell through.

From time to time, there have been sellers who have demanded that their deal be conditioned upon the successful closing of the apartment they are on contract to buy. A responsible attorney will always recommend to his client buyer not to proceed with a deal structured in this form.

WHAT TO DO IF THE BOARD OF DIRECTORS REJECTS YOUR BUYER

In a cooperative apartment sale, one standard contingency is approval by the board of directors. If the board rejects your buyer, the first thing to do is to call the president of the board or the head of the admissions committee and ask if anything can be done to cause the board to reconsider.

Sometimes the answer will be yes. Maybe the rejection was due to financial concerns, and a co-signer or a security deposit for the first year's maintenance payments will overcome the board's reservations. Maybe some financial information was missing, which, if presented, would change the outcome. All of these possibilities and more should be explored.

Another possibility is that the buyer acted in bad faith. If the buyer failed to responsibly prepare his or her board packet, or acted antagonistically in the interview, he or she may have caused the board rejection. If so, the buyer has defaulted on the contract, and the 10% deposit may be held as damages.

You should also be prepared for no response. Many boards are reticent to tell you their reasons for denial because it merely opens up a Pandora's box of potential problems and they are under no legal obligation to do so.

WHAT TO DO IF YOU HAVE A MORTGAGE CONTINGENCY PROVISION IN THE CONTRACT AND THE BUYER FAILS TO OBTAIN A LOAN

If the buyer is in compliance with all the terms of the contract, but his or her application for a mortgage has been rejected, the first step the seller should take is to insure that the purchaser complied with the provisions of the contract by submitting all required documents to the bank and putting in a bona fide application. Sometimes a rejection is due to the applicant's failure to properly comply with the bank's document requests. If so, the buyer may be in default of the contract, and the seller can keep the 10% contract deposit as damages as long as the buyer is unwilling to correct the problem.

If no bad faith was involved, the seller should get the name of the bank that rejected the prospective buyer, and ask his or her broker to call the bank or mortgage broker to determine if the buyer would qualify for a smaller loan, or if there is any way to obtain the full sum. If the bank would be willing to lend a lesser amount, the seller should consider short-term private financing to fill in the gap. The seller should also find out, by talking to a mortgage broker, if another financial institution might make the loan. Different banks have different lending policies; a rejection by one bank does not necessarily mean that another won't make the loan.

If the buyer refuses to try to find a loan through another bank or makes no other efforts to overcome this condition, it is best to give the deposit money back and find another buyer as quickly as possible. Before doing so, however, the seller should carefully read the contingency provision of the contract to determine if the buyer has strictly complied with the specified dates and forms of notice called for in this provision. If not, the buyer may be in violation of the contract, and must proceed with the purchase of the property — even in the absence of a mortgage commitment — or lose the 10% deposit.

The Challenges in Buying An Apartment

"EVERYTHING IS OVERPRICED;
THERE IS NOTHING WORTH BUYING"

When I get this response, I generally ask the buyer what a specific property is worth. Normally, they give me the price for a comparable apartment that was for sale a year ago. Accordingly, their price is not an assessment of worth, but an expression of annoyance because they realize they missed their chance last year. In seeking to determine the value of a coop or condo apartment, an appraiser will define worth as what a ready, willing, and able buyer will pay for a property, and what a seller will accept, with reference to market forces and without external restrictions. This is what is happening every day in the marketplace. Buyers are volunteering to pay and sellers are accepting their offers as the best price available at the current time.

I have found that the vast majority of people who have owned homes believe that home ownership was one of the best investments they ever made. My advice is to not wait for a better market; buy the best apartment you can afford today and begin your journey toward developing wealth. It is not a straight road — there are many hills and valleys along the way. But the only way you get there is to get on the path and begin walking.

"IT IS NOT A GOOD TIME TO BUY; THE MARKET HAS PEAKED"

As I mentioned earlier, I recently read an article warning that the real estate market was overpriced, the bubble was about to burst, and everyone was going to lose a lot of money. It was signed by Alexander Hamilton. The issue of "overpriced" property has been around since the beginning of New York City's history.

There is no question that real estate values go in cycles that run approximately 8 to 11 years. The problem is that no one really knows when a cycle will end. For instance, I purchased my apartment at the very apex of the market. It seemed as if the day after I closed on my home, real estate values came crashing down. Here I am, in the business every day, and yet I didn't see it coming. Some of the smartest people I know are real estate developers, and every one of them has a story of bad timing in the market.

I think the best thing to do is buy a home you can be happy with for at least five years — enough time to give the market a chance to fall and come back. In my opinion, there is never a good or bad time to buy a home; there are only right and wrong apartments.

"THERE ARE NOT ENOUGH CLOSETS IN THE APARTMENT"

Very few apartments in New York have adequate closet space. Developers get a better return on their investment capital if they devote more space to the main living areas than to closets. So what can a buyer do? I propose the following:

• **Identify spaces to build closets.** *Put a wall unit in the center of a living room wall and build two closets on either side which can be used as anchors for shelving. Have the doors of the closets open on the other side (which is normally a hallway or a bedroom), or place the opening on the living room side and apply a laminated- or mirror-front to the doors. Have the doors open by a push response rather than a handle. This gives a minimally intrusive look.*

• **Use armoires.** *Armoires provide extra storage space with the finished look* *of furniture, and the practical clothes-hanging storage capability of closets.*

• **Use platform furniture with storage under the cushions or mattresses.** *Many furniture stores offer beds and sofas that also provide effective and inconspicuous storage areas.*

• **Find out if the building has basement storage.** *Many buildings offer homeowners storage bins in the basement. Ask if this is available in the building you are considering. There is often no additional charge, and the storage unit is rarely reflected in the purchase price.*

• **Hire a storage consultant.** *Some storage consultants are amazingly creative in developing storage ideas for small apartments, and you can hire one to design and build storage space for you. Your real estate broker can probably give you a recommendation.*

"I ONLY WANT TO BUY A STEAL"

I respect buyers who say they want a "steal." Who wouldn't? The problem is that if an apartment is selling at an extraordinary discount, common sense says there is probably a good reason. If you think you found a steal, look closely at who is getting the better end of the deal. Frequently, it's not you. However, there are legitimate reasons why the seller might be motivated to sell at a discount — economic distress, change in family status, estate issues, or indifference. You should feel comfortable with the underlying reason motivating the discount. If you are looking for a steal, you should:

• *Make sure you have cash readily available so that, after making an offer, you can deliver your down payment quickly.*

• *Get information on buildings where you think there might be good opportunities. Review the prospectuses and the most recent financial statements. If you know the property, you will be prepared to sign a contract immediately when an opportunity arises. Speed is important.*

• *Make sure you have an attorney who can move quickly in reviewing a contract. I have even encouraged buyers to have their attorney generate the contract in order to stimulate the quickest possible response from the seller.*

• *Get pre-approval on your mortgage financing in writing. If you want a steal, you are not going to succeed if your offer has a mortgage contingency.*

You must be prepared to move quickly. As the saying goes, "the early bird catches the worm." Don't get caught up in details — you need to take risks with the belief that you will be rewarded. If you are not prepared to do this, pay a little more and consider it the cost of an insurance policy to reduce your risk exposure.

"THE APARTMENT NEEDS WORK"

There are a lot of people who prefer "fixer-upper" or "sweat-equity" apartments because they plan to change any space they buy, and don't want to pay a premium for finishings they intend to remove. The advantage of an "ugly duckling" is that the seller is giving you a discount on the price to reflect the cost involved in improving the property, and then you can make the changes that suit your needs exactly.

Years ago, real estate developers sought to market apartments as "raw space." They believed that buyers would respond favorably to the discounted price and that these apartments would sell quickly. They were wrong; many buyers were incapable of envisioning the potential of raw space. However, many others got great deals and turned the raw space into beautiful homes. Sometimes, when buyers are resistant, I propose that they get an architect and contractor to evaluate the space and the cost of construction. In this evaluation, the total price of the apartment is the "base" cost plus the improvement cost. They should give these plans, as well as their contractor's estimates, to the bank as part of their mortgage application. As long as the total estimate is within the appraised value for the improved property, banks are willing to finance the cost of improvements along with the original purchase price.

Sometimes, in a tight market, tired old apartments sell for as much as apartments in good condition. Buyers are compelled to pay top dollar because of the lack of viable alternatives.

"THE UNDERLYING MORTGAGE FOR THE COOPERATIVE CORPORATION IS COMING DUE"

A maturing mortgage is often a great opportunity, not a problem. Look at the "notes" section of the building's financial statement to find the total monthly payment for both principal and interest. Then, take the balance of the mortgage (the current portion plus the long-term portion) and divide the monthly payment by the principal. Multiply this figure by twelve to obtain the current yearly percentage of payout to principal. This figure will frequently be very high, since a maturing mortgage has a large amount of amortization (principal repayment) with every payment. When the building refinances the mortgage, the payment may go down since the principal of the loan has declined. This will cause the related payout percentage to be lower, conforming to a new payout schedule (15 or 30 years) on the lesser sum. In addition, while the principal amortization included with each payment will go down, the interest portion of the payment goes up. This means that upon refinancing your maintenance goes down and your tax deduction goes up. The moral of the story is: don't run away from a mortgage coming due.

"WHAT ABOUT ASBESTOS AND LEAD?"

Asbestos still exists as insulation on pipes in many residential buildings, including pipes within apartments. While removing asbestos might appear to be a prudent thing to do, many contractors discourage removal and recommend that asbestos be "encapsulated," a procedure wherein the pipes are enclosed in drywall. Removal is very expensive and the airborne filaments that remain in the apartment for an extended length of time after removal are dangerous.

In the 1990s, a national controversy arose regarding lead-based paint hazards. While the cost of removing asbestos contamination in the United States has been estimated at $200 billion, the estimated cost of lead removal is $600 billion. Obviously, lead is a staggering problem that has no simple, quick solution. In response, Congress passed federal legislation requiring sellers and real estate brokers to provide home buyers for dwellings built after 1978 with an informational packet about the hazards of lead in the home entitled "Protect Your Family From Lead In Your Home." I recommend that you read this packet in order to properly understand the risks.

In 1999, the City of New York enacted Local Law 38, requiring landlords to send written notices to each apartment in buildings built before 1960 to determine if any children under six reside in the home, and if any paint is peeling or cracking, which may signal a lead-based paint hazard. The landlord must also make a yearly visual inspection of apartments with young children to insure that no lead-based paint hazard exists. Where an apartment has peeling or cracking lead-based paint, the city permits the landlord to use "exclusive interim controls," which include thoroughly washing and scraping the area using prescribed procedures and repainting. In addition, the landlord must insure that all doors, cabinets and windows are adjusted so that the surfaces do not rub against each other causing paint to chip.

It is unlikely that a seller will know if a lead-based paint hazard exists, and testing is not normally performed before a sale. In any case, a federal Lead Paint Disclosure Form must be signed by the buyer as a condition to the sale of the apartment. You should assume that if the apartment was built before 1960 there is a potential lead problem, and that the exclusive interim control procedures defined by the New York City Department of Health should be used in the minimum. The guide, issued by the City of New York Department of Health, can be obtained via the Internet at **www.ci.nyc.ny.us/html/doh/html/lead/lead38.html**.

"I ONLY WANT A CONDOMINIUM"

Many buyers prefer a condominium to a cooperative, since they believe they will not have to go to a board interview and reveal their personal finances to their prospective neighbors. However, many condominiums in New York have a review process, referred to as a "right of first refusal," which can be as extensive as a coop review. Fortunately, experience has shown that the number of occasions where the condominium exercised this right of first refusal has been extremely low. I would suggest a condominium to a buyer under the following circumstances:

• **You absolutely refuse to reveal any financial information.** *Some condominiums permit this, particularly in new construction.*

• **You are buying the apartment as an investment.** *Condominiums generally have more liberal rules regarding renting than cooperatives. However, there*

*are certain situations where coops permit rentals and some buildings have
more liberal policies than others.*

• You have limited down payment cash. *You can normally purchase a condominium with a 10% down payment.*

I have analyzed the pricing difference between condominiums and cooperatives and have found, on average, for similar apartments, condominiums are approximately 30% more expensive than coops. About half of this
difference can be explained by the lower interest rate available for a condominium loan (0.5% less), and by the higher monthly charge in a cooperative relating to the cost of the building's underlying mortgage. The remaining 15% premium is for other factors including ease of transfer, flexibility in
down payment amount, and right to rent.

SHOULD I BUY A HOME WITH ALL EQUITY CASH
OR GET A MORTGAGE?

Buying a home without a mortgage obviously reduces the monthly cost of
the home since no debt payment must be made. However, given the current tax law an unforeseen wrinkle might discourage some buyers from taking the route. The current law permits a tax deduction for "original acquisition financing" which is defined as a loan to acquire your residence which is
taken at the time of closing but not later than ninety days after closing. If a
mortgage is obtained at a later time, it is deemed a replacement mortgage
and interest is only deductible to the extent of the mortgage being replaced
plus $100,000. If there was no original mortgage, nothing is being replaced
so the total principle that can have an interest deduction is limited to
$100,000.

"I SHOULD GET A BETTER DEAL
BECAUSE I'M 'ALL CASH'"

To a seller, almost every deal is "all cash." The cash comes from the buyer's
deposit or from the mortgage proceeds. Either way, the seller leaves the
closing with a check equal to his or her selling price, less closing adjustments

and the amount used to pay off his or her own mortgage. The issue that is important to a seller is "closing risk." Your purchase is more attractive to the seller if it is not conditional on obtaining a mortgage.

"I'M NEW TO NEW YORK. WHAT SHOULD I KNOW BEFORE I DECIDE TO BUY AN APARTMENT?"

Try to go to each neighborhood and attempt to evaluate its personality and how you would feel about living there. Make sure you go during the day-time and at night. Each neighborhood is different and special in its own way. Bellmarc has prepared a Neighborhood Survey Report, which I believe is very useful. It gives a quick rating and evaluation guide to many Manhattan neighborhoods, and can be found at Bellmarc's internet site, **bellmarc.com**. Another idea is to read a tourist book about New York.

After researching different areas, go to *The New York Times,* classified section and find the type of apartment you're looking for in various neigh-borhoods. Seek to get an impression of the prices in each area. You may find that the more expensive neighborhoods are not where you thought they would be.

"SHOULD I BUY IN A NEW BUILDING?"

Apartments in new buildings tend to sell for 10% to 25% more than resales. Many people feel it's worth the premium because they are not buying the headaches associated with someone else's used wares. But the situation is more complex than that. Some of the biggest headaches known to humankind are experienced by owners living in newly constructed buildings during the first two years of operation, when everyone is still trying to get the kinks out. This is particularly true if the building is unusually tall or archi-tecturally dramatic, because this technology is still actively evolving. On the other hand, most people who buy these properties are happy they did. They enjoy the efficiencies of modern systems, the larger windows, and the gen-eral feeling of new and clean. An important note: many new construction projects charge the sponsor's cost of transfer to the buyer. Make sure you clearly understand all the costs of transfer in order to properly evaluate your decision.

"SHOULD I LOOK FOR AN APARTMENT WITH A HIGH TAX DEDUCTION?"

A high tax deduction in the maintenance charge is normally due to a high interest expense relating to the underlying mortgage on the building. Therefore, the tax deduction in maintenance is merely switching the loan from being on your unit to being on the building. It's still a loan with interest just applied in a different form. I suggest that buyers should ignore the tax deductible portion of maintenance, and focus on the cash down payment amount and the monthly carrying cost when making a decision.

"WHAT ARE LOFTS AND ARE THEY GOOD FOR ME?"

In the early 1900s, New York was a manufacturing town. Large numbers of buildings were built throughout the city for small businesses producing everything from women's blouses to paper clips. Many of these buildings are now obsolete for their original uses and have been recycled as housing. These spaces display some amazing features. They normally have high ceilings, with huge windows and open environments. Many of the buildings are architectural gems, with exciting ornamentation and cast-iron finishings. Without question, some of the most incredible apartments I have ever seen were loft apartments. However, there is another side to the equation. Loft buildings are usually located in areas where there are limited neighborhood services (exceptions include Soho and the Flatiron District). During evening hours the streets are desolate, and there are few parks and other amenities. Few lofts have doormen, so loft-living lacks the security and services provided in doormen buildings. However, if you can live without a doorman, investigating loft apartments is a good idea.

"WHAT DOES IT MEAN TO BUY IN A LANDMARK DISTRICT?"

New York has many neighborhoods that are so incredibly charming, you wish you could preserve the fantasy forever. Each building seems like a historical statement referencing an age long past. The beauty of these neighborhoods didn't just happen. It requires ongoing vigilance to insure that the wonderful architecture is preserved, and the unique character of each particular neighborhood is maintained.

The City of New York has sought to protect the best of these neighborhoods by designating Landmark Districts. Under the strict rules associated with this designation, no building may be altered, demolished, or restored without a thorough and vigorous review by the New York City Landmarks Commission.

There are many buyers who love landmark districts; they believe these neighborhoods offer greater peace and tranquility, and they are pleased that the area's ambiance is protected from change. However, some of the buildings in landmark areas are caught between a rock and a hard place. They are not economically viable in their current form, yet they cannot be materially altered due to the restrictions of the Landmarks Commission. The result is that sometimes they become eyesores to the neighborhood. If a building seeks to make improvements, it does so at its own peril. The improvement will probably be exorbitantly expensive, since it must replicate historical details that are all but impossible to recreate without the services of an expensive artisan. History can be a very expensive commodity to maintain. If you are the owner of an apartment in a landmark building, you should remember that when you question the size of the next assessment.

"WHAT IS AN 'A.I.R.' BUILDING?"

A number of years ago, the city set up a special program in certain areas where there were loft apartments: the Artist in Residence or "A.I.R." program. It is intended to give special protection to artists by designating their right to live and work in these special buildings. The rules demand that the artist be in full-time pursuit of his or her occupation. The program has been notoriously abused, and the City of New York has become vigorous in reviewing applicants to minimize violations. If you really are an artist and are looking for a work/home environment, A.I.R. properties are definitely worth investigating.

"WHAT IS A PREWAR BUILDING?"

Recently, a buyer asked: "Are they still building prewar buildings?" The answer is no, because that war is over. The "war" in "prewar" is World War II. What makes prewar apartments special to many buyers is the quality of construction, which many afficionados feel is a lost art. The walls between apartments are thick enough to insure that sound stays within each unit. The floors are thick hardwood, and the moldings are large, ornamental, and frequently made of solid oak or cherry, rather than the inexpensive pine used in today's new construction projects. In addition, the exteriors have a sense of distinction and warmth. Many buyers say that prewar buildings "feel" like a home, while new construction feels cold and stark.

The disadvantages of prewar buildings are equally apparent — especially when the heat comes on and the radiator makes a knocking sound, or the shower staggers with bursts of hot and cold water. The plumbing is old, and the electrical system is usually inadequate. Worse, these problems can rarely be identified in the process of buying an apartment, because to do so would require a full engineering report, which is cost-prohibitive. When you live in a prewar building, you can all but expect that from time to time there will be an assessment to upgrade some building component. As long as you build this into your mental plan, prewar apartments are wonderful places to live. They are in such demand, you may even have to pay a premium to buy one of these apartments.

"WHAT IS A CONDOP?"

The term "condop" has been applied confusingly to New York real estate to describe the hybrid nature of a building's ownership form, and effectively has two meanings. The first is its use among real estate brokers to designate a cooperative building where there is no board approval requirement for the sale or rental of an apartment. The second meaning is the legal definition. It is a building where there is mixed use of the property, and where the space for each use receives a separate unit deed, thereby qualifying the building as a condominium. In turn, the unit deed dedicated to residential use is owned by a cooperative corporation which issues shares of stock and proprietary leases to specific apartments. Each year, homeowners receive two financial reports: the first covers the entire building as a condominium association, and the second covers the cooperative corporation owning the residential section of the building. Therefore, the shares of the cooperative have underlying ownership of the condominium unit deed for the residential segment of the building rather than a deed for the entire property.

"WHAT ARE THE ADVANTAGES AND DISADVANTAGES OF A BROWNSTONE?"

The term brownstone is a misnomer used by brokers to refer to all small buildings approximately 20 or 25 feet wide, normally on a plot running 100 feet deep. Generally these properties are walkups, and provide no doorman services. However, there are a number of wonderful features in brownstones. They are normally the cheapest properties to buy, with the lowest maintenance charges. Many of them have been divided into small studio and one bedroom apartments and are situated on tree-lined streets that offer a relatively safe, quiet existence. Some brownstones are partitioned into larger apartments that include rear gardens and duplexes. These sell extremely well, because they afford a level of privacy close to that of a full townhouse.

The downside of brownstones is that because they rarely have elevators the owners on the fourth and fifth floors may find themselves in great physical shape in a year or two, but somewhat discouraged about the relative demand for their apartment on a resale. An additional problem is management. Most of these buildings are handled by small management companies that provide minimal services. The superintendent is frequently part-time, which means he may not be around when you need him.

"WHAT DO I DO IF I WANT TO MAKE CHANGES TO THE APARTMENT I'M BUYING?"

When a buyer plans to make alterations to an apartment after the purchase, he or she must provide the cooperative corporation or condominium association with a "scope of work" letter describing the work to be performed. Depending on the extent of the improvement, the managing agent may determine that an alteration agreement is required. This agreement sets forth the terms and conditions under which the alteration may be performed, and it will normally require that the following documents be provided:

1. Architectural plans and specifications;
2. Required city building permits;
3. Proper insurance certificates;
4. Copies of any applicable contractor licenses.

Once this information is submitted to the managing agent, it is reviewed by the building's architect or engineer, and then presented to the board for approval. Usually, no work may be performed until after this approval is obtained. All costs incurred by the board for professional services related to the planned alterations must be paid by the apartment owner. In addition, it is customary that a security deposit is given to the building to be held in escrow until the alteration is complete.

If a purchaser is intent on performing a renovation in an apartment he or she is about to buy, an indication of prior approval should be sought from the board. A work letter, outlining the proposed work, should be included in the board packet material. This information will be reviewed in the context of the overall approval.

If the improvement is made after the apartment is already owned, the requirements for an alteration agreement normally remain the same. If you wish to obtain funds for the improvement by refinancing your property you will be able to increase the principal amount of your loan up to the permissable maximum of $1,100,000 and still enjoy a tax deduction on this interest as long as all the refinanced funds are applied to pay off the mortgage you replaced and the improvement to the property.

"WHAT PROBLEMS EXIST IN COMBINING TWO OR MORE APARTMENTS INTO ONE?"

Given the scarcity of large apartments, it has become very common for buyers to purchase two or more apartments and combine them to create a single larger unit. The City of New York has not objected to this, and merely requires a notification to the building department and revision of the building's certificate of occupancy. This is not a major undertaking, and a buyer should not be discouraged from combining apartments as long as there is an indication from the board that they will approve the combination. Given the level of activity to date, boards normally approve the combining of apartments unless there is some larger problem.

WHAT IS A BUYER BROKER?

When a seller employs the services of a real estate broker under an exclusive agreement, that broker is deemed to be the "Exclusive Listing Broker." When a buyer is presented by another broker to the apartment he/she is often called the "Buyer Broker." Theoretically, the Buyer Broker is an agent of the buyer and should be attempting to negotiate the best possible terms for the buyer's benefit. However, the commission paid to the Buyer Broker is derived from the commission payment made by the seller. The theory behind the payment is that the Buyer Broker is being paid in consideration for bringing a buyer to the apartment rather than for negotiating the terms of the deal. There are many in the industry who question whether this tenuous interpretation would suffice under judicial scrutiny and believe that buyers should be cautioned that the party who pays the commission is controlling the outcome.

ESCROWS AS A CONDITION TO A SALE

Where a cooperative board has reservations on the financial qualifications of a prospective buyer, a common alternative to rejection is to require the buyer to deposit with the coop a sum to be held by it for additional protection. The amount is normally a minimum of six months maintenance but is commonly as large as one or even two years. Normally, after the stated duration has expired the deposit agreement requires that the buyer request a return of the funds. However, the Board in its sole discretion can't refuse if it has continuing concerns.

Escrow deposits are also common in condominiums where the Condominium Board will refuse to sign a waiver of its right of first refusal unless there is an escrow deposit agreement.

Currently, there is lively debate among real estate attorneys as to whether escrow deposits are legal. From a practical point of view, for the prospective buyer about to close on a sale, paying the escrow deposit is a better choice than other alternatives.

"SHOULD I USE THE INTERNET?"

The internet has become an important medium for brokers to communicate with buyers about their property offerings. Most firms now have sites that are normally the name of the company and "dot-com." Many of these sites provide an array of information about market conditions and the firm. There are also a number or internet search engines that have good broker participation. The best is The New York Times site: **nytimes.com**. A buyer should view the internet as an additional useful tool to help gain a fuller appreciation of the market.

Epilogue

I frequently tell salespeople that a buyer is not buying four walls, a ceiling and a floor. The buyer is purchasing a dream. He or she is seeking to find a sense of fulfillment, and the purchase of a new apartment represents the next plateau of personal achievement. The new home symbolizes an expression of his or her lifestyle and vision of the future. My advice to sales associates is not to focus just on logic and facts; purchasing a property must feel right to the dream as well as to the dollar.

I tell sellers that there are no foolish buyers. A buyer usually must have a substantial income to purchase the home being sold. A person making that kind of money is a shrewd businessperson, an accomplished professional, or a talented manager. I caution sellers to remember that the buyers are as smart as they are; that's why they are considering purchasing the seller's apartment. Sellers should consider what they would do in all their wisdom. The key to convincing buyers is not to fool them, but to educate them.

I tell buyers that every seller is looking to make a profit. One of the reasons they purchased a home was to make money on the resale. The issue is not how much money the seller is making, but for the buyer to hope that he or she will make as much money when it is their turn.

I tell both buyers and sellers that real estate brokers have families and dreams just like they do. We want to be excellent in our service to clients and customers so that someday we can participate in the dream of owning a home, too. And that's the beauty of it all — the real estate salesperson's ultimate dream is to be his or her own buyer, or his or her own seller.

Glossary

Adjusted Sales Price The price on the contract, less all selling costs recognized and permitted under the Internal Revenue Code.

Amendment In the course of converting a building to homeownership, the sponsor may alter his or her offer by filing an amendment to the Offering Plan. Amendments also may occur after the date of conversion if there are new offers made to tenants still in occupancy, and to provide pertinent financial disclosure information about the sponsor or material investors.

Appraiser An expert responsible for evaluating the worth of a selected property. Generally, an appraisal is performed on behalf of a bank in the process of evaluating a borrower for a mortgage. The purpose of an appraisal is to insure that the property, which is security for the loan, has adequate value to meet bank requirements.

Amortization The payment of principal on a liability (including a mortgage), or the write-off of a non-depreciable asset over a scheduled term of years.

Assessment An extraordinary payment called for by the board of directors of a cooperative corporation or condominium association for the purpose of making a capital improvement, or to provide some other essential service for which funds in the reserve account are inadequate.

Asset Something you own that has value.

At Risk Under the United States Internal Revenue Code, an owner of investment property either must be personally responsible for the indebtedness on real estate, or the debt must be issued by a financial institution in order for the full purchase price of the property to qualify as the tax basis in determining depreciation.

Balloon Mortgage A mortgage which matures with a balance still owed at the end of the term.

Board Approval A condition in the standard cooperative sales contract requiring that the buyer obtain approval from the board of directors of the cooperative corporation as a prerequisite to completing the sale.

Buyer Broker A broker who represents the buyer in effectuating a purchase. Normally, in residential real estate transactions, the buyer broker shares the commission received by the listing broker, who represents the seller.

Bylaws The rules by which the cooperative corporation operates, including those regulating elections, officers, and authorizations.

Capital Gain The seller's gain on the sale of an asset used in a trade or business or for investment, including real estate. This gain is taxed at varying rates depending on whether the asset was held for a short-term (less than one year — ordinary rates), medium-term (one year to eighteen months — 28%), or long-term (over eighteen months — 20%).

Carrying Cost Rule A rule used by banks to evaluate borrowers for loans. It gives the maximum percentage of a borrower's income that the bank will find acceptable to carry the loan and related housing costs. This rule is used in conjunction with the Debt/Equity Rule.

Co-brokerage An arrangement between two brokerage firms to share a commission. Normally used when one broker is the seller's exclusive listing agent, and the other broker represents the buyer.

Collateral The security put up in exchange for a loan, which can be taken by the bank if the loan goes unpaid.

Commitment Letter A letter issued by a bank which legally binds it to provide funds as specified subject to the written terms and conditions.

Common Charge The monthly charge levied by a condominium to cover the cost of maintaining the common areas and services.

Condominium A building in which ownership has been partitioned into unit interests. Each apartment owner receives a unit deed.

Conforming Loan A mortgage issued within the framework of FNMA (Fannie Mae) guidelines in terms and amount.

Contract Vendee Sale When a seller transfers beneficial rights — including the right of possession and obligations of ownership — to the purchaser, and agrees to close at a future date under definite terms. Ownership can be transferred for tax purposes prior to the transfer of title.

Conversion A change in ownership status. For example, rental housing may be converted to cooperative or condominium ownership. Such changes must conform to guidelines determined by the laws of New York State.

Cooperative A building owned by a corporation in which each apartment is allocated shares of stock, as well as a proprietary lease.

Debt/Equity Rule A rule used by banks requiring that a borrower invest a minimum amount of equity cash (usually 10% to 25% of the purchase price) as a condition to obtaining a mortgage. This rule is used in conjunction with the Carrying Cost Rule to determine how much mortgage money a bank will lend.

Debt Service The cost of carrying a loan (usually through monthly payments), including the payment of interest and principle.

Default An act performed by either the buyer or seller that breaches the contract of sale and permits a claim for damages.

Depreciation The expensing of the original cost of an asset, plus any qualified improvements, over its scheduled life as defined by the Internal Revenue Code. Depreciation deductions are permitted only for assets held for the production of income, or used in a trade or business. The current term for depreciating residential real estate is 27.5 years

Escrow A sum of money held by one person in trust for another, for the purpose of assuring performance under an agreement. Normally, in a residential real estate sale, the attorney for the seller is the escrow agent for the deposit money securing the deal until closing.

Equity The difference between what something is worth and any loans secured by that asset (i.e., the value of a home less the outstanding mortgage).

Exclusive Agency Agreement An agreement between a broker and a seller designating the broker as the seller's sole agent for the purpose of selling his or her property. This agreement does not preclude the owner from effectuating a sale him or herself.

Exclusive Right to Sell Agreement An agreement between a broker and a seller designating the broker as the seller's sole representative for the purpose of selling property. In contrast to an exclusive agency agreement, under an "exclusive right to sell agreement" a commission is due to the broker even if the apartment is sold directly by the owner.

Financing A loan secured by personal property. The stock and lease of a cooperative corporation constitute such personal property, and a loan secured by these instruments is referred to as a financing loan. Generally real estate brokers refer to these financing loans as mortgages because they operate in the same manner even though, technically, they are not.

Flip Tax A levy issued on the transfer of ownership by a cooperative corporation or condominium association against either the buyer or seller.

House Rules Building rules regulating the conduct and responsibilities of each homeowner as they effect the building's common areas and services.

Insider Rights Special rights offered to tenants occupying apartments in a building in the process of converting to home-ownership, giving them the exclusive right to buy their apartments for a limited period of time, normally at a discounted price.

Installment Sale A property sale in which the purchaser pays the purchase price over a period of years. The seller recognizes gain for tax purposes by the proportion of the profit (determined by the profit divided by the net sales price of the asset) received on each payment as it is received.

Interest Rate Spread The differential between the retail interest rate charged to a borrower and the wholesale rate accepted by Wall Street when acquiring home mortgage loans. Spread is profit to the bank.

J-51 A New York City program giving tax breaks for the substantial rehabilitation of an existing property. The program provides for an abatement of tax on a formula based on the level of improvement, and an exclusion from additional tax due to the change in use of the property.

Jumbo Loan A mortgage issued in an amount exceeding the threshold stipulated under FNMA (Fannie Mae) regulations for a conforming loan.

Landmark The designation given to a building or neighborhood which is under New York City protection for purposes of preservation.

Landmarks Commission A governmental agency assigned responsibility for recommending properties and neighborhoods to be landmarked, and insuring that landmarks are properly preserved.

Letter of Adequacy A letter (usually issued by a managing agent) found in the Offering Plan of a building converting to cooperative or condominium ownership, affirming that the income and expenses, as expressed in the proposed operating budget, are adequate to cover the costs of running the building. This expert evaluation is required by the New York State Martin Act.

Letter Of Reasonable Relationship A letter issued by an expert (usually a real estate broker) affirming that the allocation of shares or unit percentage interest in a cooperative or condominium conversion is rational and reasonable in accordance with New York State law.

Liability A debt or claim you owe.

Like Kind Exchange An exchange of similar property, as defined in the Internal Revenue Code, which can be performed without recognition of gain.

Listing The term used by brokers for an apartment for sale after it has been "listed" by the broker in its system.

Listing Broker The broker who represents the interests of the seller in effectuating the sale of his or her property.

Maintenance The monthly charge levied on owners by a cooperative corporation to cover the building's operating costs, real estate taxes, and the debt service on the building's underlying mortgage.

The Martin Act The New York State law regulating the conversion of properties to cooperative or condominium ownership. Also referred to as Section 352eee and 352eeee of New York State's General Business Law.

Mortgage A loan secured by real estate.

Mortgage Banker Performs services similar to a mortgage broker. However, a mortgage banker is also legally permitted to lend its own funds.

Mortgage Broker A real estate professional who represents an array of banks seeking to issue mortgages. The mortgage broker meets with a customer, assists with the application, and effectuates the mortgage process on behalf of the borrower and the bank. Generally, in the case of residential mortgages, the mortgage broker is paid a fee by the bank for this service.

Negative Amortization When a loan permits the borrower to make a payment less than the full amount required to cover the interest charge on the open balance, and the shortfall is added to the mortgage principal.

Net Worth Your assets, less your liabilities.

Offering Plan See "Prospectus."

Open Listing An apartment for sale for which the owner has not signed an exclusive agreement with any real estate broker.

Passive Loss A loss generated by investment real estate when real estate is not the taxpayer's primary business. Loss in excess of income may not be fully recognized for tax purposes in the year it was incurred.

Perfecting a Loan When a loan is issued against personal property, it is recorded in the county clerk's office against the name of the borrower. The recording process *perfects* a security position against the collateral.

Phantom Gain A sale of real estate in which income is recognized for tax purposes but no money has been received correlating to the gain amount. This can occur when the property's basis has been depreciated below the property's mortgage amount.

Points Payment made to a bank as consideration for issuing a mortgage, usually based on a percentage of the loan amount.

Profit Exemption Current tax rules permit the profit on the sale of a primary residence to be tax exempt for up to $250,000 for an individual, or $500,000 for a married couple.

Proprietary Lease The lease issued by a cooperative corporation to each tenant-stockholder prescribing his or her right to occupy a specific apartment, and his or her general obligations as an owner and tenant.

Prospectus Also referred to as the Offering Plan or Black Book. The prospectus is a document issued by a sponsor in the process of converting a building to cooperative or condominium ownership. It is intended to provide "full disclosure" of all relevant facts associated with evaluating an investment in the property.

Recapture When investment real estate has been depreciated for tax purposes, the gain on the sale includes a "recapture" of the previously written-off depreciation as gain. In certain cases, this can result in a tax liability that exceeds the cash received. See "Phantom Gain."

Recognition Letter A letter from the cooperative corporation board of directors recognizing the secured rights of a lender to the shares of stock and the proprietary lease on a specific apartment.

Recording Registering the ownership, lien, or claim of a party to a specific parcel of real estate with the local county.

Rental The possession, but not ownership, of a property for a limited duration of time under defined terms and conditions.

Right of First Refusal A condition contained in many condominium master deeds which permits the board to review any party seeking to purchase or rent an apartment, and to refuse the applicant if it so desires. If the board refuses the applicant, it must thereafter purchase or rent the apartment under the same terms and conditions stipulated in the contract.

Section 421 A A New York City tax program intended to stimulate new construction by permitting a phase-in of the real estate tax over a period of ten years.

Sponsor The party initiating the conversion of a property from single ownership to cooperative or condominium ownership.

Schedule A A list, in the Offering Plan, of all the apartments being sold in a newly-constructed building or one that is undergoing conversion. It presents allocated shares or unit percentage interest, room count, and other material cost elements, including the projected maintenance charge and the tax-deductible portion of the maintenance.

Schedule B The projected cost of operating a cooperative or condominium during its first year of operation. Found in the Offering Plan.

Standing Mortgage An interest-only mortgage with no principal reduction over time. See "Balloon Mortgage."

Subject to Financing A clause in the contract of sale for a cooperative apartment stipulating that the agreement is conditioned upon the buyer obtaining financing from a financial institution in an agreed upon amount.

Unsold Shares Shares of stock in a cooperative corporation transferred to the sponsor at the completion of the conversion process. The sponsor normally gets special rights to rent and/or sell these shares (representing specific apartments) without board approval.

Index

G

GBL section 352eee, 147
GBL section 352eeee, 147
Gross Income, 185
guarantors, 118

H

high maintenance, 192
high tax deduction, 208
house rules, 106

I

income approach to valuation, 157
insider rights, 157
installment sale, 138
internet, 57, 63, 185, 186, 191, 206,
    207, 213
INVESTING, 154–162

L

land leases, 104
Landmarks Commission, 209, 221
landmarks designation, 209, 221
lead, 205
liability, 222
lofts, 208
loss, selling at a, 195

M

market approach to valuation, 158
Martin Act, The, 221

mortgage banker, 222
mortgage broker, 24, 223
MORTGAGES AND FINANCING,
    107–116
    90% financing, 111
    amortizing loans, 108
    application fees, 24
    balloon mortgage, 160
    bridge loan, 195
    carrying cost rule, 218
        back end percentage, 108
        front end percentage, 108
        housing cost rule, 107
    collateral, 219
    commitment letter, 25, 94, 219
    conforming loans, 115, 219
    contingency, 200
    debt service, 220
    debt/equity ratio, 33, 110
    Debt/Equity Rule, 219
    default, 220
    financing, 23, 220
    fixed rate, 24
    heavy leverage, 111
    income ratios, 107
    jumbo loans, 115, 221
    legal fees, 24
    mortgage, 222
    mortgage associations, 114
        Fannie Mae, 114, 115
        Freddie Mac, 114
    moving costs, 129
    negative amortization, 113, 223
    perfecting a loan, 223
    points, 24, 114, 223
    portfolio lenders, 115

BELLMARC
The Real Estate Resource

BELLMARC IS LOOKING FOR MOTIVATED PEOPLE TO ENTER ITS SALES TRAINING PROGRAM

Bellmarc is always looking for motivated applicants to join its sales training program and then to enter into a career as a sales associate in one of its six neighborhood offices located throughout Manhattan.

If you are exploring a career change and see commission income as an opportunity to earn what your efforts truly deserve, then we encourage you to contact us. We desire individuals with the following qualities:

1. You must sincerely like people.

2. You must have a college degree.

3. You must want a full time position.

We are seeking people with excellent life experience. A background in real estate is not required.

The Bellmarc Training Program requires that you listen to and study a series of audiocassette tapes, and that you learn the material in our sales manual. Following that, you must complete a round of written exams. We conduct weekly teaching seminars which you are encouraged to attend.

There is no up-front cost for the training. It is provided to ensure your success in the business, from which both you and Bellmarc will reap rewards in the form of commissions earned from sales.

If you have a deep desire to learn, enjoy helping people, and strive for excellence, then you should consider a career as a salesperson at Bellmarc. We are eager to discuss the exciting opportunities available with us.

Please call our personnel director at 212-252-1900, extension 350.

Notes

Notes

FINDING THE RIGHT LOAN CAN BE EASY.

THAT'S WHY WE'RE IN BUSINESS.

We offer the loans of **more than 80 major banks, at better rates** than you can obtain from the banks directly. You **save money and time** and we personalize the process.

One phone call gives you all the information you will need on pre-approvals, fixed and adjustable rate loans, jumbo loans and non-income verification loans. Whether you're interested in a coop, condominium, loft or townhouse, we deliver.

EASY. CONTACT THE EXPERTS AT HMAC.

HOME MORTGAGE ACCEPTANCE CORP
28 West 44th Street • Suite 1114 • New York, NY 10036
Phone: 212-997-7280 • Fax: 212-997-7335

SERVING BELLMARC BROKERS AND THE RESIDENTIAL REAL ESTATE COMMUNITY FOR OVER A DECADE.

HOME MORTGAGE ACCEPTANCE CORP.
HMAC

Loans arranged through third party providers.

Registered Mortgage Broker, NYS, NJ & CT Banking Departments.